MACMILLAN ACADEMIC SKILLS

Skillful

Listening&Speaking

Student's Book

3

Authors: Mike Boyle & Ellen Kisslinger
Series Consultant: Dorothy E. Zemach

2   CONTENTS

Contents

To the Student

Academic success requires so much more than memorizing facts. It takes skills. This means that a successful student can both learn and think critically.

Skillful gives you:

- Skills for learning about a wide variety of topics from different angles and from different academic areas
- Skills you need to succeed when reading and listening to these texts
- Skills you need to succeed when writing for and speaking to different audiences
- Skills for critically examining the issues presented by a speaker or a writer
- Study skills for learning and remembering the English language and important information.

To successfully use this book, use these strategies:

- **Come to class prepared to learn** This means that you should show up well-fed, well-rested, and prepared with the proper materials (paper, pen, textbook, completed homework, and so on).
- **Ask questions and interact** Learning a language is not passive. You need to actively participate. Help your classmates, and let them help you. It is easier to learn a language with other people.
- **Practice** Do each exercise a few times, with different partners. Memorize and use new language. Use the *Skillful* Digibook to develop the skills presented in the Student's Book. Complete the additional activities on your computer outside of class to make even more progress.
- **Review your work** Look over the the skills, grammar, and vocabulary from previous units. Study a little bit each day, not just before tests.
- **Be an independent learner, too** Look for opportunities to study and practice English outside of class, such as reading for pleasure and using the Internet in English. Find and then share information about the different unit topics with your classmates.

Remember that learning skills, like learning a language, takes time and practice. Be patient with yourself, but do not forget to set goals. Check your progress and be proud of your success!

I hope you enjoy using *Skillful*!

Dorothy E. Zemach
Series Consultant

Welcome to *Skillful*!

Each *Skillful* unit has ten pages and is divided into two main sections: listening skills and speaking skills.

Listening

The listening skills section always comes first and starts with a *Discussion point* to lead you in to the unit topic.

There are then two listening texts for you to practice your listening skills on. There are activities to practice your global listening skills and your close listening skills, as well as opportunities to critically examine the ideas in the texts. Key academic vocabulary is presented on the page so you can see essential terms to learn.

Vocabulary skills also give you the chance to develop the ways in which you learn and remember vocabulary from the listening texts.

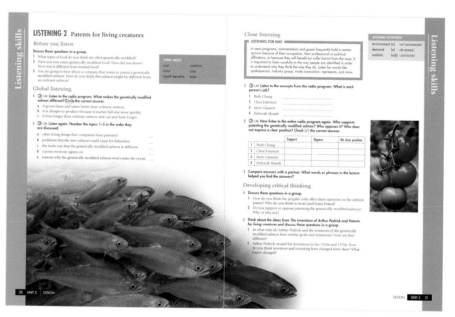

Speaking

The speaking section has three main parts: grammar, pronunciation skills, and speaking skills. You can find information on each of these in boxes on the page and these give essential information on these skills. At the end of this section there is a speaking task for you to put the ideas from the texts and the skills from the speaking section into practice.

The final page in the unit focuses on study skills which will help you to achieve academic success. Some of these pages come from *The Study Skills Handbook* by Stella Cottrell, while others are engaging scenarios for you to read and reflect on.

Using *Skillful* gives you everything you need for academic success.

Good luck!

Introduction

Each *Skillful* Student's Book comes with a code in the back of the book that gives you free access to the accompanying Digibook. The Digibook encourages a more interactive and engaging learning environment and is very simple to access. Just go to www.skillfuldigibooks.com, and follow the step-by-step instructions to get started!

The first time you access the Digibook you will need an Internet connection, but after this it is possible to work offline if you wish.

Digital Student's Book

This contains all the same content as your printed Student's Book, but you can use it on your computer, enabling easier navigation through the pages, a zoom function to create better student focus, and a personal annotation resource for helpful classroom notes.

Skillful Practice

You can either complete the extra activities as you go through the Digital Student's Book via the interactive icons, or you can find them all in one place in the *Skillful* Practice area. Here you will find a variety of activities to practice all the new skills and language you have learned in the Student's Book, including vocabulary, grammar, and skills-based activities.

There are also additional productive tasks and video activities linked to the unit topics.

If you complete any of the extra activities while you are online, your score will be recorded in your markbook so that your teacher can track your progress. If you work offline your scores will be stored and transferred to your markbook the next time you connect.

Whether online or offline, in the classroom or on the move, the *Skillful* Digibook allows you to access and use its content while encouraging interactive learning and effortless self-study.

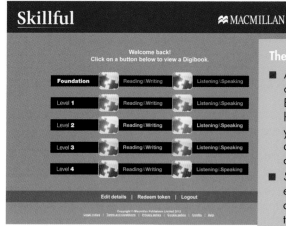

The Digibook contains:

- A digital version of the Student's Book, complete with hotspots that take you to embedded audio and other additional content;
- *Skillful* Practice, with extra interactive activities for you to review what you have learned, including video-based activities.

The Digital Student's Book also contains lots of hotspots that link to additional content not in your printed Student's Book:

- Audio files for all of the reading texts
- Useful language to support discussion activities
- Dictionary definitions for the *Academic Keywords*
- Unit checklists so you can monitor how well you are progressing through the course.

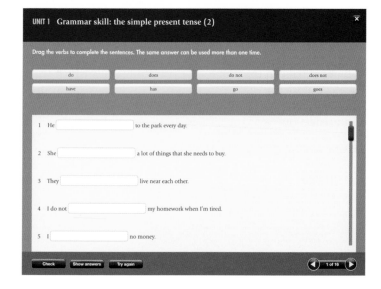

Identity

LISTENING	Listening for main ideas: key words
	Recognizing phrases used to introduce examples
VOCABULARY	Suffixes
SPEAKING	Expressing interest in ideas you hear
PRONUNCIATION	Using thought groups

Discussion point

Discuss these questions with a partner.

1 How would you describe your own personality? How do you think others might describe you?

2 Think of a friend. How would you describe the friend so that your partner could identify him or her?

3 What are first impressions of other people usually based on? In your experience, how often are first impressions accurate? Share examples.

Vocabulary preview

1 (Circle) the correct meanings of the words in bold.

1 The main reason for going to college is to **attain** a good job after graduation.

    a succeed in getting something   **b** make even

2 Children are more physically **flexible** than adults.

    a continuing   **b** able to bend easily

3 No two people walk in an **identical** way.

    a in position   **b** exactly the same

4 I don't like having to write my **marital status** on a form.

    a opinion   **b** official information about whether you are married

5 I think countries should **permit** entry without a passport.

    a engage   **b** allow

6 The family **structure** in my country is very strong.

    a organization   **b** substance

7 Even very small babies have their own **unique** personality.

    a one of a kind   **b** intense

8 The best way to **verify** someone's identity is with a photo ID.

    a check   **b** treat with respect

2 Work with a partner. Discuss whether you agree with the sentences.

LISTENING 1 Life events

Before you listen

You will hear a talk show discussing answers to the question *What was a life event that affected your identity?* Check (✓) four events you think people are likely to mention.

☐ becoming a parent   ☐ getting a driver's license   ☐ getting married

☐ being selected for a sports team   ☐ getting a job   ☐ graduating

☐ discovering a personal ability   ☐ getting engaged   ☐ winning an award

☐ doing well on an entrance exam

Global listening

> ### LISTENING FOR MAIN IDEAS: KEY WORDS
>
> Listening for key words and phrases will help us understand a speaker's main ideas. If the main idea is: *There are many life events that affect our self-identity,* key words are: *life events* and *self-identity.*
>
> A speaker may signal a key word by:
>
> - saying the word and then defining it, e.g. *self-identity, by that I mean ..., that is ..., that means ..., / In other words ...*
>
> - repeating it throughout the presentation.

1 🔊 1.02 **Listen to the TV interview about life events. What major life events were mentioned? Complete the chart.**

Interviewee	Event
1	
2	
3	
4	

ACADEMIC KEYWORDS

achievement	(n)	/əˈtʃivmənt/
enable	(v)	/ɪnˈeɪb(ə)l/
typical	(adj)	/ˈtɪpɪk(ə)l/

2 **Work with a partner. What key words did you hear? Take in turns to summarize what you remember about each of the life events you heard described.**

Close listening

🔊 1.02 **Listen again. Write *T* (true) or *F* (false) based on the radio show.**

1 The first identity change was connected to a family role. ___

2 The woman now has three children. ___

3 The student trained for a couple of years. ___

4 The second student felt his life event gave him independence. ___

5 The last interviewee was helping at her grandson's school. ___

6 All the interviewees talked about common major life events. ___

Developing critical thinking

Discuss these questions in a group.

1 Which of the life events you heard described do you think had the biggest long-term effect on changing the person's identity? Explain your reasons.

2 What experiences have you had of trying something for the first time, and liking it? Why are some people more willing to try something new than others?

USEFUL LANGUAGE

adventurous   risk taker

cautious   sensible

LISTENING 2 Beyond the ID card

Before you listen

Discuss the questions with a partner.

1 What information is on your ID card?

2 What other information about yourself that isn't on your ID card would you want to share if you were introducing yourself?

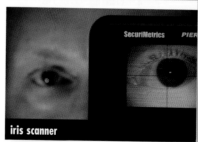

iris scanner

Global listening

1 🔊 1.03 **Listen to the lecture. Check (✓) the types of identification that are mentioned.**

☐ student ID   ☐ voice recognition

☐ passport   ☐ DNA testing

☐ PINs   ☐ iris pattern scan

☐ fingerprinting   ☐ driver's license

☐ face scan

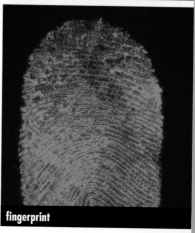

fingerprint

2 Answer the questions.

1 How does the speaker define biometric information?
2 What is one major disadvantage of photo IDs?
3 Which type of identification does the speaker think is the most reliable?

Close listening

RECOGNIZING PHRASES USED TO INTRODUCE EXAMPLES

In addition to identifying main ideas, it is important to be able to identify which phrases introduce examples of the main ideas: *for example ..., such as, ... for instance, ... a couple of examples are ..., to elaborate further ... The first type of biometric information is ...*

1 🔊 1.03 **Listen again.** Circle **the answer to each question.**

1 Which of the following details about photo IDs are NOT mentioned?
   a nationality   c size
   b gender   d identification number
2 Which two reasons are given for why passwords aren't 100% reliable?
   a can be forgotten   c can't be letters only
   b can be long   d can be stolen
3 The main problem with fingerprints is that the skin on a fingertip:
   a has patterns   c is flexible
   b is unique   d is smooth
4 The first step in using voice recognition is that someone records:
   a their address   c a passphrase
   b their name   d their birthdate
5 A disadvantage of DNA testing is that the lab can only determine:
   a a 100% match   c the DNA
   b two samples   d a match probability
6 Because the iris of the eye is flat, it's easy to:
   a change over time   c be flexible
   b create an accurate video image   d move

2 🔊 1.03 **Listen again. Decide if the sentences are *T* (true) or *F* (false). Change the false statements to make them true.**

1 Because 3-D fingerprint scanners use light, not touch, they are more reliable.
2 Voice recognition is reliable because features like pitch and rhythm vary from person to person.
3 Only a very small amount of DNA features are the same for everyone.
4 The shape of the iris in the eye is used to determine someone's identity.
5 Voice recognition is used for automated passport crossings because it is the most reliable.
6 The speaker believes the use of biometric information is likely to increase.

ACADEMIC KEYWORDS

determine	(v)	/dɪˈtɜrmɪn/
establish	(v)	/ɪˈstæblɪʃ/
physical	(adj)	/ˈfɪzɪk(ə)l/

Developing critical thinking

1 Discuss these questions in a group.

1 In addition to crime scenes, what are other places and situations in which the reliability of biometric identification is especially useful?

2 Imagine a world where there were no formal means of identification. What might be the pros and cons?

2 Think about the ideas from *Life events* and *Beyond the ID card* and discuss these questions in a group.

1 Which do you think identify a person more: major life events, or the information on an ID card? Give reasons.

2 Which parts of our physical identities change, and which parts remain the same, as we go through life?

Vocabulary skill

SUFFIXES

A suffix is a group of letters added to the end of a word that usually changes the part of speech. Knowing the meaning of common suffixes will help you to develop a rich vocabulary.

Sometimes there can be two noun forms with different meanings.

Identity is the concept of who we are while *identification* is usually the act or result of identifying someone or something:

*Life events that effect one's **identity**.*

*It's not 100% reliable as a form of **identification**.*

1 Add the correct ending for these nouns and adjectives and put them in the appropriate column. Add others you know.

> **Nouns:**
> inform-   national-   probab-   recogni-   reliab-   vari-   verific-
> **Adjectives:**
> attain-   manage-   structur-

Common adjectival endings		Common noun endings	
related to (= -al, -ive)	capable of (= -ible, -able)	state or result (= -ation, -tion, -sion)	quality of (= -ty, -ity, -ility, -ance, -ence)
personal	*responsible*	*identification*	*identity*

2 Complete the paragraphs with the correct form of the words in the box.

flexible	inform	nation	probable	verify

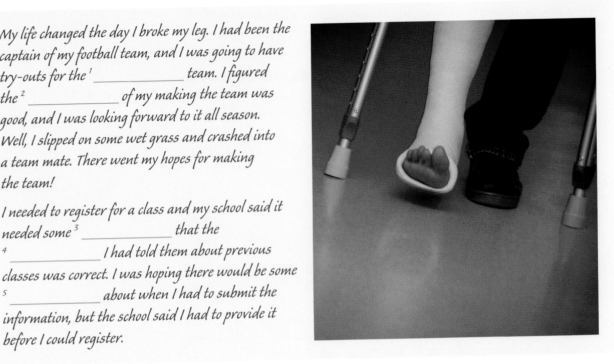

My life changed the day I broke my leg. I had been the captain of my football team, and I was going to have try-outs for the ¹ _____ team. I figured the ² _____ of my making the team was good, and I was looking forward to it all season. Well, I slipped on some wet grass and crashed into a team mate. There went my hopes for making the team!

I needed to register for a class and my school said it needed some ³ _____ that the ⁴ _____ I had told them about previous classes was correct. I was hoping there would be some ⁵ _____ about when I had to submit the information, but the school said I had to provide it before I could register.

SPEAKING Sharing a self-introduction

You are going to practice using conjunctions to join ideas, expressing interest in ideas you hear, and using thought groups to make your ideas clear. You are then going to use these to share introductions about yourself.

Grammar

CONJUNCTIONS: COORDINATORS AND SUBORDINATORS

Conjunctions are used to link ideas in order to communicate the relationship between them.

To link ideas of equal status, use coordinators such as: *and, but, or, so, yet, and so, either, neither*.

To link ideas of unequal status, use subordinators to express various relationships such as:

purpose/result: *so that, to*	reason: *as, because*	contrast: *while, whereas*
preference: *rather than*	manner: *as, as though*	time: *while*

In general, *and* is used to mean 'in addition', and *but* is used for contrast, but they can also be used as follows:

for a sequence:	*Khalil finished class and went to a coffee shop.*
contrast:	*That man is tall but his brother is short.*
unexpected:	*He has short legs, and yet he is a very fast runner.*

1 Read the conversation. (Circle) the correct conjunction.

A: I have an opportunity to study abroad next year **but** / **while** I can't decide where to go. I can either go to Germany **and** / **or** New York.

B: Well, in New York you could speak English **so that** / **whereas** in Germany you might have more language difficulties.

A: My classes in Germany would all be in English **but** / **so** I would be fine. My brother had a great time **so that** / **while** he was in school there.

B: I would decide based on what you want to study **yet** / **rather than** which country you want to live in.

2 Discuss the questions with a partner. Think about the conjunctions you use.

1 What was an important choice you have had to make?
2 What do you like to do while you are relaxing at home?
3 Compare yourself to a friend or a family member. How are you alike? How are you different?

Speaking skill

▌ **EXPRESSING INTEREST IN IDEAS YOU HEAR** ▌

During a conversation or informal discussion, it's important to let other people know that you are paying attention and that you are interested in what they are saying.

<u>Making comments</u>

Wow! Really? Hmmm, You're kidding! That's/That sounds interesting.
I can't believe it! That's incredible/fantastic!

<u>Repeating part of what you heard</u>

You said 'Don't do that'?

<u>Asking follow-up questions</u>

When a person pauses, you can ask questions to get more detail, e.g.
How *did you do that?*
Why *did you go there?*
When *was that?*
Who *taught you that?*

1 🔊 1.04 Listen to four people speaking. ~~Cross out~~ the response that would **not** be appropriate.

1 Why did you stop? / That's a shame. / You're kidding!
2 What was it about? / Really? / I can't believe it.
3 Wow! What a coincidence! / It was a guy you didn't recognize? / How did you know who it was?
4 You lost it? / Oh no! / That sounds interesting.

2 Practice the conversations from exercise 1, with appropriate intonation, choosing one of the possible responses. Continue the conversations for a couple more lines.

Pronunciation skill

USING THOUGHT GROUPS

A thought group is a group of words in a sentence that are pronounced together as a unit by pausing briefly between them.

There are no fixed rules for thought groups. Thought groups are often based on grammatical units:

I made the swim team. (a short sentence = one thought group)

I made the swim team / at my school. (the prepositional phrase is a second thought group)

1 🔊 1.05 **Read the sentences. Draw a line (/) between the thought groups. Compare with a partner. Listen and check, then repeat.**

1 What do identification cards tell us about who someone is?
2 An ID card from India will include about 16 personal details.
3 I hope to be a skillful doctor some day.
4 The lab used several samples before they got a good match.
5 The patterns in the iris of the eye are unique to every individual.

2 **Work with a partner. Take turns reading aloud, using thought groups. Then discuss whether you agree with the ideas.**

We all have hopes and dreams. Part of achieving a dream, for example, becoming a civil engineer, is being able to envision your future self in that identity. One consideration is your skills and abilities. Evaluate what you can do now, what you know, and what skills and knowledge you still need to learn to attain your goal. Then make a plan for how to learn what you need to know. Your plan will help you feel in touch with your future identity.

3 **Continue the conversation with a partner. Try to use thought groups and remember to express interest. Then change over.**

A: Have you had any experiences that affected your self-identity?

⬇

B: [Tell your partner about an experience.]

⬇

A: [Respond to what you hear and ask another question.]

⬇

B: [Answer the question.]

4 **Now have similar conversations starting with the following prompts.**

Have you thought about what you want to do for a career?
Do you have any hobbies?
How many people are there in your family?

SPEAKING TASK

Work with a partner to explore what 'Aha!' moments are and prepare a self-introduction that includes past experiences and decisions.

Audience: peers/classmates
Context: small group study session
Purpose: self-introduction, team-building

BRAINSTORM

Read the paragraph and the questions below.

> Our identity develops through the life experiences we have. One type of experience is an 'Aha!' moment, an instant when you suddenly understand something for the first time. It may be something simple, like a concept in a mathematics class, suddenly getting a clear idea about how to solve a bigger problem, such as what school to go to, or what career choice to make. In an 'Aha!' moment people suddenly feel they have learned something new about themselves that will change their life in some way.

1 Think about any 'Aha!' moments you've had in class or doing your homework, during which you suddenly understood something clearly for the first time.
2 What are common big decisions people have to make at different points in their lives? Make a list.
3 What are some useful strategies for weighing the pros and cons of a situation in order to try to reach an 'Aha!' moment and knowing what to decide?

PLAN

Work alone. Prepare notes on self-introduction. Include:
- brief information about your hobbies, interests, and your family
- any major past experiences that you feel affected your identity
- any 'Aha!' moments when it suddenly became clear to you what the right decision or solution to a problem was.

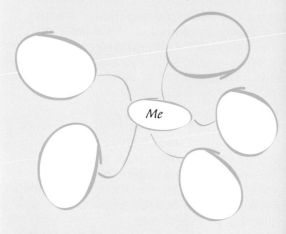

Me

SPEAK

Work with a new partner. Take turns presenting your self-introductions. As you speak, use conjunctions, and pay attention to thought groups to make your ideas clear. As you listen, use words and phrases to express interest. Ask follow-up questions to find out more details about what your partner tells you.

SHARE

Work with a different partner. Take turns sharing what you learned about your previous partners.

Identifying your current skills

by Stella Cottrell

Think about something you do well, a difficulty you overcame, or a personal achievement, no matter how small. It might be success in your exams, skill in a particular sport, learning to drive, or being accepted at college.

What did you do to create the conditions that led to success? Which skills, attitudes, and qualities did you demonstrate? Did you practice? Did you urge yourself on in a particular way? Did you find people to help? Or did you just believe you could do it? Look at the example below for some ideas.

Example: The beautiful garden

Supposing one year your garden or a window box was absolutely beautiful. How did that happen?

Many small things may have brought about a perfect outcome. For example, maybe you watered the plants very carefully, depending on the weather. If so, you used powers of *observation* and *deduction*. You may have worked in the garden in the rain, when you wanted to stay indoors. Here you *kept in mind your long-term goal* for the garden, showing *dedication* and *perseverance*.

You may have *selected* some new plants from a wide range of options, to match your garden conditions. You *followed specific instructions* on how to grow them. You probably did *research* by reading gardeners' books and seed packets, talking to other gardeners or watching television programs. You may have purchased special fertilizer and pots, or prepared the ground in a certain way, or trimmed the leaves at particular times: such care requires *attention to detail*, *time management* and *task management*.

All these skills are relevant to study. Whether your experience is in cooking, riding a bicycle, sport or bringing up children, you are likely to have developed a range of strengths such as those described in the example above. The important thing is to recognize which qualities and abilities you already have so that you can draw on them when you need them.

Activity

Skills from experience

Write down all the elements that go into something you have done well, as in the example of the garden. Note the skills, qualities and attitudes you identify in yourself.

Were you surprised to discover how many skills you have already? Do you tend to underestimate or overestimate your skills?

By doing the 'Skills from experience' exercise, you probably discovered you have more skills than you thought. If not, go through the exercise with someone who knows you well. Most people already have qualities and skills which they can adapt to study in Higher Education.

- Students who enter university from school have the benefit of recent study experience and established study habits.
- Mature students often have practice in managing time and responsibility, show perseverance, and can evaluate other people's views. These are valuable assets when studying.

Design

LISTENING	Listening for rhetorical questions
	Listening for bias
VOCABULARY	Word families
	American and British English: collocations with *have*
SPEAKING	Giving examples
PRONUNCIATION	Weak form of *that*

Discussion point

Work with a partner and discuss the questions.

1 What are some inventions you use every day? Make a list.
2 What do you think life was like before these inventions? What problems did the inventions solve? Did they create any problems?
3 How do you think inventors get their ideas? Do they usually work alone or in groups? In what ways are inventors different from ordinary people?

Vocabulary preview

1 Complete the paragraph below with the words in the box.

| benefits | creative | devices | genetically modified |
| industries | invention | patent | research | solutions |

Humans have been creating tools, gadgets, and other
(1) _____ for many thousands of years, ever since the
(2) _____ of fire-starting tools roughly 400,000 years ago. Like fire,
the best inventions are (3) _____ to our most important problems;
they offer huge (4) _____ and make life easier and happier. In
addition, inventions such as the automobile developed into massive
(5) _____ that employ millions of workers. These companies
spend billions on (6) _____ to develop new gadgets, vehicles,
medicines, and more recently, (7) _____ plants and animals.
Because the (8) _____ and hardworking people who make these
discoveries are so important to us, inventors can ask governments to
grant them a (9) _____. This document describes an invention and
gives its inventor the exclusive right to sell it.

**2 Compare answers with a partner. How would you define each word?
What part of speech is each word?**

LISTENING 1 The inventions of Arthur Pedrick

Before you listen

Work with a partner. Look at the pictures of inventions and discuss the questions.

1 What do you think each invention is?

   a _____

   b _____

   c _____

2 Which of the inventions do you think exists today?

A few inventions of Arthur Pedrick

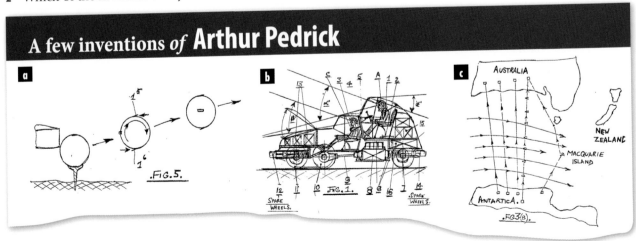

Global listening

1 🔊 1.06 **Listen to a British speaker describing the inventions. Circle the correct answer.**

1 What kind of talk is this?
   a a sales presentation   **b** a news report   **c** a lecture
2 How long have the people known each other?
   a a day   **b** a few months   **c** a year
3 Who speaks the most in the passage?
   a the professor   **b** Marco   **c** Pedrick

2 🔊 1.06 **Listen again. What do the inventions in the pictures do? Write a, b, or c next to the correct description. (Some descriptions will not be used.)**

1 It's an underwater train system between Australia and Antarctica. _____
2 It's a car you can drive from the back seat. _____
3 It's a system for moving snow from Antarctica to Australia. _____
4 It's a golf ball that flies three times farther than a normal ball. _____
5 It's a car you can drive underwater. _____
6 It's a golf ball you can steer in the air. _____

3 **Compare answers with a partner. What words or phrases in the lecture helped you find the answers?**

Close listening

> ■ **LISTENING FOR RHETORICAL QUESTIONS** ■
>
> Rhetorical questions are common in academic discussions and debates. They sound like normal questions, sometimes with stronger intonation, but they are not real questions and the speaker does not expect an answer. Rhetorical questions are used to state a point the speaker believes is obvious, and to express attitudes such as surprise, doubt, and agreement.
>
> Normal question: *Does anyone care?* (= Maybe some people care; I want to know the answer to this.)
>
> Rhetorical question: *Who cares?* (= No one cares.)

🔊 1.07 **Work with a partner. Listen to some questions from the lecture and check (✓) the rhetorical ones. How can you tell that they are rhetorical?**

1 Professor: Who can tell me what these inventions are? _____
2 Ling: Wow, who knows? _____
3 Professor: What golfer hasn't had that happen? _____
4 Brian: So who is Arthur Pedrick? _____
5 Professor: Sorry, your name is …? _____
6 Marco: Why patent them? I mean, what's the point? _____

Developing critical thinking

Discuss these questions in a group.

1 Which of Pedrick's inventions do you admire the most? Why?
2 Which of the inventions does the professor think is the most important? Why?
3 What makes an idea or invention good?

ACADEMIC KEYWORDS

practical	(adj)	/ˈpræktɪk(ə)l/
prevent	(v)	/prɪˈvent/
produce	(v)	/prəˈdus/

USEFUL LANGUAGE

groundbreaking	profitable
innovative	unique
life-saving	useful

LISTENING 2 Patents for living creatures

Before you listen

Discuss these questions in a group.

1 What types of food do you think are often genetically modified?
2 Have you ever eaten genetically modified food? How did you know? How was it different from normal food?
3 You are going to hear about a company that wants to patent a genetically modified salmon. How do you think this salmon might be different from an ordinary salmon?

THINK ABOUT:

cost	nutrition
color	size
health benefits	taste

Global listening

1   1.08 **Listen to the radio program. What makes the genetically modified salmon different? Circle the correct answer.**

  a It grows faster and tastes better than ordinary salmon.
  b It is cheaper to produce because it reaches full size more quickly.
  c It lives longer than ordinary salmon and can stay fresh longer.

2   1.08 **Listen again. Number the topics 1–5 in the order they are discussed.**

  a other living things that companies have patented   ____
  b problems that the new salmon could cause for fishermen   ____
  c the main way that the genetically modified salmon is different ____
  d a point everyone agrees on   ____
  e reasons why the genetically modified salmon won't enter the ocean ____

Close listening

LISTENING FOR BIAS

In news programs, commentators and guests frequently hold a certain opinion because of their occupation, their professional or political affiliations, or because they will benefit (or suffer harm) from the issue. It is important to listen carefully to the way people are identified in order to understand why they think the way they do. Listen for words like *spokesperson*, *industry group*, *trade association*, *represents*, and more.

ACADEMIC KEYWORDS

environment	(n)	/ɪnˈváɪrənmənt/
demand	(n)	/dɪˈmænd/
realistic	(adj)	/ˌriəˈlɪstɪk/

1 🔊 1.09 **Listen to the excerpts from the radio program. What is each person's job?**

1 Ruth Chang   _____

2 Clara Emerson   _____

3 Steve Clauson   _____

4 Deborah Shatah   _____

2 🔊 1.08 **Now listen to the entire radio program again. Who supports patenting the genetically modified salmon? Who opposes it? Who does not express a clear position? Check (✓) the correct answer.**

		Support	Oppose	No clear position
1	Ruth Chang			
2	Clara Emerson			
3	Steve Clauson			
4	Deborah Shatah			

3 **Compare answers with a partner. What words or phrases in the lecture helped you find the answers?**

Developing critical thinking

1 **Discuss these questions in a group.**

1 How do you think the peoples' jobs affect their opinions on the salmon patent? Who do you think is most (and least) biased?

2 Do you support or oppose patenting the genetically modified salmon? Why or why not?

2 **Think about the ideas from *The inventions of Arthur Pedrick* and *Patents for living creatures* and discuss these questions in a group.**

1 In what ways do Arthur Pedrick and the inventors of the genetically modified salmon have similar goals and intentions? How are they different?

2 Arthur Pedrick created his inventions in the 1960s and 1970s. How do you think inventors and inventing have changed since then? What hasn't changed?

Vocabulary skill

WORD FAMILIES

Many English words can easily change into adjectives, verbs, and nouns. This is usually done by changing the end of the word. It is useful to learn and remember common endings of adjectives, nouns, and verbs, as they are very frequent in academic English.

1 Complete the table with the correct noun, verb, and adjective forms.

	Verb	Noun	Adjective
1	invent	_____ , _____	_____
2	_____	patent	_____
3	_____	solution	
4		gene	_____
5	concern	_____	_____

2 Complete the sentences with the correct noun, verb, or adjective form of the word in parentheses.

1 Thomas Edison, the _____ (invent) of the light bulb, also _____ (invent) the phonograph.
2 A _____ (patent) device may only be sold by its inventor.
3 Are you _____ (concern) about genetically modified food?
4 The _____ (invent) of writing happened over 5,000 years ago.
5 There are now _____ (gene) tests for a variety of diseases.
6 Solar power may be the _____ (solve) to the energy crisis.

Thomas Edison

AMERICAN AND BRITISH ENGLISH: COLLOCATIONS WITH *HAVE*

Many collocations use *have* in British English but take different verbs in American English. Also, some are expressed simply as verbs in American English.

British
have a look/guess/shower
have a think/laugh/word

American
take a look/guess/shower
think/laugh/talk (to someone)

3 Complete the questions in British English.

1 Can I have a ___*look*___ at the photos on your phone?
2 Do you usually have a _____ in the morning or before bed?
3 What do you watch on TV if you want to have a _____ ?
4 Do you know how old I am? Have a _____ !
5 Can I borrow your car tonight? Have a _____ and let me know.
6 Can I have a _____ ? I'd like to know your opinion of this course.

4 Work in pairs. Ask and answer the questions in exercise 3. Ask the questions again in American English.

SPEAKING Presenting the pros and cons of an invention

You are going to learn how to use defining relative clauses to give more information about a noun, how to say relative clauses with the weak form of *that*, and how to give examples. You are then going to use these skills to describe an invention and its pros and cons.

Grammar

DEFINING RELATIVE CLAUSES

We often use defining relative clauses to give more information about a noun. They are especially common when giving definitions, explaining processes, and describing inventions. Relative clauses begin with a relative pronoun (*who*, *that*, or *which*).

Form	Example
In a subject relative clause, the word after the relative pronoun is usually a verb.	*They want to patent a genetically modified salmon that/which **grows** faster than normal.* *Arthur Pedrick was the man who **invented** an underwater bicycle.*
In an object relative clause, the word after the relative pronoun is usually a noun or pronoun. This person or thing is doing something to the noun before the relative clause.	*He invented a golf ball that/which **you** can steer in the air.* (you steer the ball)
In an object relative clause, the relative pronoun can be left out.	*This is the invention (that/which) I was telling you about.*

1 Each of these sentences has one mistake. Circle the mistake and correct it.

1 The person which invented the zipper must be very rich by now.

2 The salmon they that developed grows twice as fast as a normal fish.

3 The company is developing a new phone runs on solar power.

4 There is a genetically modified tomato which it has genes from a fish to resist cold.

5 Companies that are suing each other over patents more and more these days.

2 Match the words to make sentences. Add a relative pronoun.

1 Arthur Pedrick invented a tunnel _____ … __
2 There are many advantages to a fish _____ … __
3 Thomas Edison was the inventor _____ … __
4 One invention _____ … __
5 The inventor _____ … __

a changed the way we learn is the printing press.
b could send water from the Amazon to the Sahara desert.
c companies can raise in half the normal time.
d has the most patents is an Australian named Kia Silverbrook.
e probably had the biggest impact on 20th century life.

3 Compare answers with a partner. In which sentence can you leave out the relative pronoun? Why?

Pronunciation skill

WEAK FORM OF *THAT*

In relative clauses, the pronunciation of the word *that* is often 'weak' and sounds like /ðət/. It can be difficult to hear this difference, but it is important to listen for it.

What's that? (strong form)

It's an invention that really changed the way we live. (weak form)

1 🔊 1.10 **Listen to the sentences from *Patents for living creatures*. Circle the weak forms of *that*.**

1 They started with genetically modified plants: corn, tomatoes, things like **that**.

2 Clara Emerson is a spokesperson for the Future Food Institute, a group **that** represents the biotech industry.

3 What makes this salmon special is it has a gene **that** lets it grow faster.

4 **That**'s all well and good, but it raises a very interesting question for the patent office.

2 🔊 1.10 **Now listen again and repeat.**

Speaking skill

GIVING EXAMPLES

In order to express your ideas clearly and convincingly, it is important to give examples. Many learners of English use the phrase *for example*, but research shows this expression is used too often. The expressions below are more frequently used in academic English.

An example of … is …   *A prime example of this is …*

… is a classic example of …   *…, to name one example.*

1 **Complete the sentences with an expression from the box above.**

1 The Incas are a prime _____ an advanced culture that never invented writing.

2 The wheel _____ classic _____ of an important prehistoric invention.

3 The drawbacks of cell phones include the potential risk of cancer, to name _____.

4 Mary Anderson, the creator of the windshield wiper, _____ an _____ of an early female inventor.

2 **Work in groups. Take turns giving examples of the things below. Try to give reasons and extra information.**

1 an invention that changed history

2 the positive and negative effects of television

3 something that wasn't possible before electric lights

4 something that a cell phone can't do yet

5 an invention that comes from your country

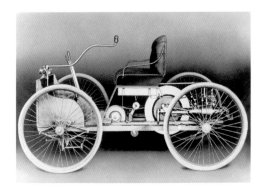

SPEAKING TASK

You are going to present the pros and cons of an invention.

Audience: teachers and students

Context: classroom presentation

Purpose: present the pros and cons of an invention

Speaking skills

BRAINSTORM

Work with a partner. How have the inventions below changed the way we live? Use the words in the box or your own ideas.

communication	crime	eating habits	energy	entertainment
the environment	fitness	free time	friendship	health
privacy	school	sleep	stress	work

PLAN

1 🔊 1.11 Listen to a short talk about the pros and cons of the light bulb. Match the lines from the talk with the stages of the talk.

1 Describe the invention ___
2 Talk about its benefits ___
3 Talk about its negative aspects ___
4 Summarize your opinion ___

a *Electric lights have improved our lives in many ways. A prime example of this is public safety.*

b *Even though there are definitely problems that light bulbs can cause, overall it's impossible to imagine life without them.*

c *This is an invention that uses electricity to light up a room.*

d *There are also changes that aren't as positive. To cite one example, people stay up later and get less sleep.*

2 🔊 1.11 Listen to the talk again. Notice the use of definite relative clauses, the weak form of *that*, and expressions with *example*.

3 Choose an invention and prepare a short talk about its pros and cons. Follow the stages in exercise 1.

SPEAK

Work in groups. Give your talk to the group. Listen to your group members' talks and suggest additional points they can make.

SHARE

Find a new partner. Tell him or her about two interesting talks you heard.

the light bulb (Thomas Edison, USA, 1879)

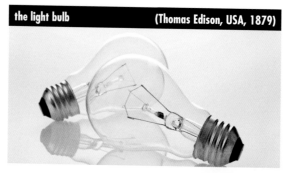

the cell phone (Martin Cooper, USA, 1973)

the Internet (US Government, 1969)

the automobile (Gottlieb Daimler, Germany, 1889)

STUDY SKILLS Taking notes effectively

Getting started

Discuss these questions with a partner.

1 When you take notes in class, what do you write down?
2 Do you write your notes only in English, only in your first language, or both?
3 Do you use charts, tables, or other ways to organize your notes?
4 Do you write down your thoughts, reactions, and questions about the lecture?

Scenario

Read the scenario and try to think of three things Ling could do to take notes more effectively.

Consider it

Look at these tips for taking notes effectively. Which ones does Ling already do? Which do you think can help Ling take better notes?

1 **Listen for key points** Don't worry about writing down every word of the lecture, but be sure to write down the main ideas.
2 **Watch the board** If your professor puts a fact, key term, or diagram on the board, you should probably copy it in your notes.
3 **Write down what the professor emphasizes** Many professors will specifically tell students to write down key information, or to make sure that they remember it.
4 **Paraphrase** Try to put the professor's ideas in your own words. This will help you understand the lecture better.
5 **Don't worry about complete sentences** Write down key phrases to help you remember the information. Don't worry about writing full sentences.
6 **Use charts and tables** For example, if a lecture is about the pros and cons of an idea, make a chart with the pros in one column and the cons in another.
7 **Write down questions** If anything isn't clear, make a note of this so you can ask questions at the appropriate time.

Over to you

Discuss these questions with a partner.

1 Which of the things above do you already do?
2 Which of the tips do you think will be most useful to you?
3 What are some other ways that you take notes effectively in class?

Ling is a second-year Engineering major, and her classes are very challenging. Her professors cover a lot of material very quickly, so she knows that it is important to take good notes. In every lecture, her goal is to write down every word her professor says so she can memorize it later. In addition, she always copies down anything her professor writes on the board, as well as anything the professor tells the class to put in their notes. Sometimes she doesn't understand the professor's ideas but she just writes down the words and hopes she can figure it out later. Many of her lectures are in English, so she tries to take notes in English. She finds this frustrating, however, because she is used to writing her notes in complete sentences, and she sometimes makes grammar mistakes.

Thought

LISTENING	Listening for summaries
	Listening for reasons and explanations
VOCABULARY	Collocations with *do* and *make*
SPEAKING	Giving reasons
PRONUNCIATION	Disagreeing

Discussion point

Discuss these questions with a partner.

1 What are some different ways that people use their brains? Make a list.
2 What are some ways that you can tell what other people are thinking? Make a list.
3 Would the world be a better place if everyone knew exactly what other people were thinking? Why or why not?

Vocabulary preview

1 Match the words from the box with the definitions.

| accurate | automatically | behavior | experiment |
| instinct | lie detector | reasoning | researcher |

1 a natural tendency to behave in a particular way that people and animals are born with: _____

2 correct or true in every detail: _____

3 a piece of equipment used for checking whether someone is telling the truth: _____

4 the way a person or animal acts: _____

5 the process of thinking in an intelligent way: _____

6 someone who studies or collects facts about something:

   _____

7 a scientific test to find out what happens in particular conditions:

   _____

8 without thinking about it: _____

2 Complete the sentences with your own ideas. Discuss your ideas with a partner.

1 You need good **reasoning** skills to work as a …

2 Medical **researchers** should spend more time studying …

3 People usually take **lie detector** tests when …

4 When I need an **accurate** weather report, I usually …

5 One task I can do **automatically** is …

LISTENING 1 Catching lies in the brain

Before you listen

You are going to listen to a news report about lie detectors. How can you tell when someone is lying? Make a list of signs. Discuss with a partner.

Global listening

▮ LISTENING FOR SUMMARIES ▮

Summarizing information is an important skill that you will need in your classes, in tests, and in your work. In lectures and news reports, the key information is often summarized near the beginning or near the end. Listen for cues such as *summarize, overview, introduction, conclusion*, and *to sum up*. These often mean that the speaker is going to give a summary.

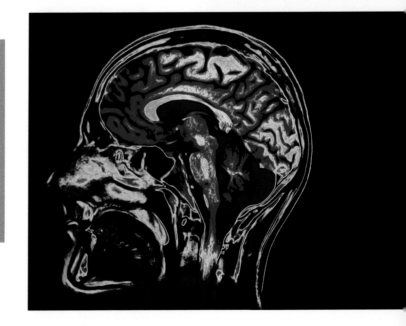

1 🔊 1.12 **Read the summaries below. Then listen to the news report on a new kind of lie detector. Check (✓) the summary that best matches the news report.**

Summary 1 ☐

For over 100 years, people have used a lie detector called the polygraph. It measures stress and is usually very accurate. The new test is called the fMRI. It measures both stress and brain activity. However, many experts believe it isn't as accurate as the polygraph.

Summary 2 ☐

People have used lie detectors for many years. The most common lie detector is a polygraph, which measures stress and is not very accurate. The new lie detector is called the fMRI. It measures activity in the part of the brain people use to tell lies. It is more accurate, but it also has problems.

2 Where in the news report can you hear a summary of this information?

Close listening

1 🔊 1.12 **Listen to the news report again and write *T* (true) or *F* (false).**

1 The fMRI lie detector can read a person's thoughts. ___
2 Good liars can beat a polygraph because they don't feel stress. ___
3 The caudate is a part of the brain that you use when you lie. ___
4 The fMRI lie detector is 100% accurate. ___
5 It is possible to use the fMRI on an uncooperative person. ___
6 It may be possible to beat the fMRI test. ___
7 You can increase your caudate activity by doing math in your head. ___

2 What words and phrases from the news report helped you find the answers?

Developing critical thinking

Discuss these questions in a group.

1 Do you think this new kind of lie detector is a good idea? Why or why not? Make a list of good points and bad points.
2 When do you think it is appropriate to use this technology? When is it not?

ACADEMIC KEYWORDS		
connect	(v)	/kəˈnekt/
function	(n)	/ˈfʌŋkʃ(ə)n/
measure	(v)	/ˈmeʒər/

USEFUL LANGUAGE
accuracy
law enforcement
national security
protect someone's feelings
privacy
white lies

LISTENING 2 Animal intelligence

Before you listen

Work in groups. How intelligent are animals? Which of these things do you think animals can do? Which animals can do them?

- communicate
- solve simple math problems
- make and use tools
- recognize faces
- travel long distances and find their way back
- your own idea

Global listening

LISTENING FOR REASONS AND EXPLANATIONS

Giving reasons and explanations is an important part of academic work, especially when people are discussing scientific theories, explaining their ideas, or interpreting the results of an experiment. You will often hear key words such as *since, so, as,* and *because* when people give reasons. Expressions such as *it's possible that …* and *it could mean that …* are often used to give explanations.

1 🔊 1.13 **Listen to the lecture on the intelligence of crows. Check (✓) the information the speakers mention.**

   a The crow in the video never reached the food. ___

   b The crow in the video made a hook. ___

   c In the same experiment, chimpanzees were not able to make tools. ___

   d It's possible that the crows were only copying behavior. ___

   e Crows may be 'programmed' to make tools. ___

   f Researchers didn't repeat the experiment with other crows. ___

   g Crow brains are much larger than pigeon brains. ___

ACADEMIC KEYWORDS		
behavior	(n)	/bɪˈheɪvjər/
explanation	(n)	/ˌekspləˈneɪʃ(ə)n/
summary	(n)	/ˈsʌməri/

2 **Which of the statements you checked in exercise 1 are reasons why crows probably have intelligent thoughts? Which are explanations for why crows do *not* have intelligent thoughts?**

Close listening

🔊 1.13 **Listen to the lecture again. Circle the correct answer to complete the sentences.**

1 The professor believes we **can / can't** directly observe the crow's thoughts.

2 Researchers have observed wild crows making tools from **leaves / stones**.

3 The crow in the video had **already / never** seen metal wire before the experiment.

4 The same crow in the video bent the wire **once / nine times** out of ten.

5 A different crow bent the wire **once / nine times** out of ten.

6 Crows and pigeons **are / are not** about the same size and weight.

Developing critical thinking

1 Discuss these questions in a group.

   1 How much more research needs to be done before scientists can say definitely that New Caledonian crows have intelligent thoughts?

   2 How are people and animals similar and different? Make a list.

2 Think about the ideas from *Catching lies in the brain* and *Animal intelligence* and discuss these questions in a group.

   1 Do you think the technology in *Catching lies in the brain* could be used to learn more about animal cognition? Make a list of reasons why or why not.

   2 We can often guess what people are thinking simply by observing them and using common sense. Do you think today's technology is an improvement over observation and common sense? Will it ever be?

Vocabulary skill

COLLOCATIONS WITH *DO* AND *MAKE*

The verbs *do* and *make* are used in numerous expressions in English. Many words and phrases can only go with one of these two verbs and not the other. It is useful to keep a record of collocations you learn with *do* and *make*, as well as with other common verbs such as *get* or *have*.

*One part controls memory, another **does math**, another **makes decisions**, another **makes plans**.*

1 Which words in the box go with *do*? Which go with *make*? Put each word in the correct column.

> business   a decision   an exception   an experiment
> a favor (for someone)   a mistake   a plan   progress
> ~~research~~   someone wonder   the right thing
> your homework

do	make
research	

2 **Complete the questions with the correct form of *do* or *make*. Then ask and answer the questions with a partner.**

1 Are you _____ research on anything in your classes these days?

2 Do you think scientists will _____ progress on the question of animal intelligence?

3 If you need to _____ a big decision, what do you do?

4 When was the last time someone _____ an exception to the rules for you?

5 Who was the last person you _____ a favor for?

6 Would you like to _____ business abroad one day?

3 **Write three sentences about the topics below. Use collocations with *do* and *make*.**

- lie detectors
- animal intelligence
- things you wonder about
- or your own idea

SPEAKING Discussing the results of an experiment

You are going to learn how to use adverb clauses to present contrasting information and show the order of events, how to give reasons in a discussion or debate, and how to use your tone of voice to express disagreement politely. You are then going to use these skills to discuss the results of an experiment.

Grammar

ADVERB CLAUSES OF CONCESSION; REDUCED ADVERB CLAUSES OF TIME

Adverb clauses of concession

Adverb clauses of concession use words such as *though, although, even though, whereas,* and *while* to add contrasting information to a sentence. An adverb clause is a dependent clause and must go with a main clause with a subject and a verb.

- We use *though, although,* and *even though* to show ideas that are contrasting but related.

  Although the crow might be thinking, *we just don't know for sure.*

- We use *whereas* and *while* to compare two different people, things, or situations.

  While the polygraph measures stress, *this new technology actually looks inside your brain.*

Reduced adverb clauses of time

If an adverb clause of time (*after, before, when, while*) has the same subject as the main clause, you can reduce the adverb clause by removing the subject and putting the verb in the *-ing* form.

While visiting these islands, *researchers observed crows making tools.* (reduced form)

*After **the researchers** returned home, **a journalist** interviewed them.* (can't be reduced)

1 (Circle) the correct word to complete the sentences.

1 He was arrested for the robbery **while / even though** he passed a lie detector test.

2 Crows are able to make tools, **though / while** pigeons can fly long distances and find their way back.

3 **Although / Whereas** I love cats, I don't believe they really have intelligent thoughts.

4 **Though / After** failing with the straight wire, the crow bent it to make a hook.

5 Some people can look you right in the eyes **though / while** lying to you.

2 Combine the sentences. Use adverb clauses and the words in parentheses. When possible, use a reduced adverb clause. Sometimes more than one answer is possible.

1 Scientists have learned a lot about the brain. There is much we still don't know. (though)

   Though scientists have learned a lot about the brain, there is much we still don't know.

2 Some animals make tools. They are not as sophisticated as human tools. (although)

3 Researchers studied crows. Researchers thought only chimpanzees used tools. (before)

4 Chimpanzees are very smart. Other animals are not as intelligent. (whereas)

5 Many companies rely on lie detectors. Lie detectors are not 100% accurate. (even though)

Speaking skill

GIVING REASONS

When you contribute your ideas to an academic discussion, your opinions will be clearer and more convincing if you also give reasons for them. When giving reasons, we frequently use clauses with words such as *because, since, as,* and *so.*

Really good liars can beat the test **because** *they just don't feel that stress.* (= this is the reason why really good liars can beat the test)

As and *since* are used in lectures and other more formal or academic situations.

As *the crow had never seen metal wire before, those explanations are less likely.*

More informally, we can express the same idea using a clause with *so* in the middle of the sentence.

The crow had never seen metal wires before, **so** *these explanations are less likely.*

1 Use the information to write sentences. Put the word in parentheses in the most appropriate place in the sentence.

1 animals can't speak our language / it is difficult to understand their minds (since)

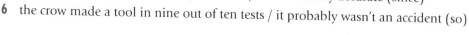

   Since animals can't speak our language, it is difficult to understand their minds.

2 humans aren't the only ones who use tools / crows can also do this (as)

3 fMRI scanners are large and expensive / they aren't widely used yet (so)

4 polygraph tests aren't accurate / some people can lie without feeling stress (because)

5 the fMRI actually looks inside your brain / it is extremely accurate (since)

6 the crow made a tool in nine out of ten tests / it probably wasn't an accident (so)

THOUGHT

2 Work with a partner. Do you agree with the ideas below? Take turns giving reasons for and against each one. Use the words and expressions from the box. Then try to give additional reasons.

1 Mammals are more intelligent than birds.
2 People should never tell lies.
3 Rainy weather is a bad thing.
4 It's a good idea to go to university.
5 Watching television is bad for you.
6 The brain is the most important part of the body.

Pronunciation skill

DISAGREEING

In class and in academic contexts, you will need to politely express disagreement in discussions and debates. Many people use a higher intonation and speak a bit more slowly to show politeness when they disagree. They may stress certain words in order to soften the disagreement, while at the same time putting *less* stress on words such as *no*, or *disagree*.

A: *So some birds are just as intelligent as people.*

B: *Um, no, I'm not sure I **COMPLETELY** agree.*

1 🔊 1.14 Listen to the lines from *Catching lies in the brain* and *Animal intelligence*. Notice the higher tone of voice. Circle the stressed words.

1 **A:** These machines can read your thoughts – do I have that right?
  B: Well, no, not exactly.

2 **A:** Wow, over 95%. So I guess we'll be seeing this in police stations and airports soon.
  B: Well, probably not too soon.

3 Thank you, Alison, for that very clear summary. **I just want to disagree on one point.**

2 🔊 1.14 Now listen again and repeat the lines in bold.

3 Work with a partner. Take turns to read the false statements below aloud to your partner. Your partner disagrees. Use a polite, higher tone of voice and emphasize words that soften the disagreement.

1 People don't use their brains when they lie.
2 Only humans can make and use tools.
3 Most people begin university at the age of fifteen.
4 People will probably be living on the moon in five years.
5 Crows are smarter and bigger than all other birds.
6 Most people have never told a lie.

SPEAKING TASK

In pairs, discuss the results of an experiment.

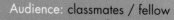

Audience: classmates / fellow researchers in a scientific context

Context: classroom / scientific research facility; discussion/ debate of research findings

Purpose: to discuss/debate what the results of an experiment mean

BRAINSTORM

1 *Collective intelligence* is the theory that a group can be smarter than any of its individual members. Do you think the situations below are examples of collective intelligence? Can you think of more?

 1 A professor asked his class to guess how many jellybeans were in a jar. No individual student guessed correctly, but the average of all of their guesses was 98% correct.

 2 On the TV game show *Who Wants to Be a Millionaire?* contestants can ask the audience to vote on the answer to a trivia question. The audience's choice is correct 91% of the time.

2 Read the information about how bees choose a new home. Do you think this is an example of collective intelligence? Tell a partner.

American researchers gave a group of 4,000 bees a choice of five boxes in which to start a new hive. Four of the boxes were too small, but one of them was the perfect size. This is what the researchers observed:

- Most of the bees stayed in a group and didn't go to any of the boxes.
- A small number of 'scout' bees left the group and found each of the boxes.
- When a scout bee returned from a box, it did a 'waggle dance', after which other scout bees went to look at the box.
- So far, there were only a few bees at each of the five boxes. As soon as about 15 scout bees gathered at one of the boxes, one of the scouts returned to the group and did another dance.
- At this point, all of the 4,000 bees followed the scout back to the box and they made their hive there.
- The bees' choice was the perfectly-sized box.
- In later experiments, different groups of bees also chose the best box.

PLAN

1 🔊 1.15 Listen to two people discussing the bee experiment. Check (✓) the points they mention.

 a The bees chose the best place for their hive.   ____

 b The bees had a 20% chance of picking the best place at random.   ____

 c The wind could have pushed the bees to the box.   ____

 d In later experiments, the bees also chose the best box.   ____

 e Most of the bees never saw any of the boxes before the group 'decided'.   ____

 f Even among the scout bees, most of them only saw one or two of the five boxes.   ____

 g You can't measure collective intelligence with a brain scanner.   ____

 h Individual bees have very tiny brains.   ____

2 🔊 1.15 Listen to the conversation again. Notice how the speakers:
- use adverb clauses of concession
- use reduced adverb clauses of time
- give reasons
- use their tone of voice to disagree politely.

3 Which reasons in exercise 1 suggest bees have or don't have collective intelligence?

SPEAK

Discuss the experiment with a new partner. Do you think bees have collective intelligence? Why or why not? Use the points in exercise 1 or your own ideas.

SHARE

Work in groups. What opinion do most people have? What are the strongest reasons for that opinion?

Memory thrives on organization

by Stella Cottrell

Activity

1   Read List A for 15 seconds, then cover it.

2   Say a nursery rhyme (to stop yourself practicing the list).

3   Write down the words you remember.

4   Check List A and note down your score. Now do the same with List B, including the underlined words. Even if you did not do well with the first list, have a go.

List A			
plum	elbow	giraffe	caravan
puppy	banana	foot	apple
pony	cherry	barge	bungalow

List B			
Fruit	Animal	Home	Body
plum	giraffe	house	foot
banana	puppy	apartment	knee
apple	donkey	bungalow	elbow
cherry	pony	caravan	hand

You probably remembered many more items from List B. List B is more memorable because:

- grouping similar items together helps recall
- using group headings helps recall
- being able to see that there are only four types of information gives the task manageable boundaries
- many of the items on List B were also in List A — and going over information again helps recall.

Organising information into pyramids

Concept pyramids (see example below) organize associated information into hierarchies. They are excellent memory aids.

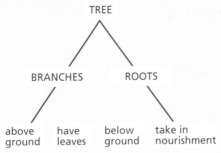

In an experiment in 1969, Bower and other psychologists asked a group of people to learn 112 words. The words were grouped and linked meaningfully, as in List B above, and organized into four pyramids. People remembered 100% of the words by the third attempt.

By contrast, a second group of people were given the same words, also arranged into pyramid shapes, but this time with the words randomly assigned to each pyramid — they were not meaningfully (or semantically) linked. The second group remembered only 47% of the words by the third attempt.

This suggests the importance of both:

- linking information meaningfully, *and*
- organizing ideas into hierarchies or concept pyramids.

Fire

LISTENING	Listening for cues to distinguish facts and opinions
	Listening to understand a sequence of events
VOCABULARY	Synonyms
SPEAKING	Changing the topic and returning to it
PRONUNCIATION	Using intonation to express feelings and attitudes

Discussion point

Discuss these questions with a partner.

1 What are five words you associate with 'fire?' Were the words mostly positive, negative, or neutral?
2 When was the last time you were near a fire? What was the reason for the fire? Why do you remember it?

Vocabulary preview

1 **Read the sentences. Circle the correct meanings of the word in bold.**

1 These animals have **adapted** to life in some of the hottest places in the world.
   a changed behavior   b lost

2 Scientists are always finding out more evidence about the lives of our **ancestors**.
   a behaviors   b people related to you who lived long ago

3 The usual way to **extinguish** a wood fire is to put water on it.
   a analyze carefully   b make a fire stop burning

4 A fire in Chicago in 1871 **destroyed** 17,000 buildings and left 90,000 people homeless.
   a consisted   b damaged completely

5 A fire can have a huge **impact** on a community if many homes burn down.
   a aspect   b effect or influence

6 There is a clear **link** between burning fossil fuels and global warming.
   a dilemma   b connection

7 It's often easier to **maintain** a familiar routine, than to change to a new one.
   a keep   b get

8 It's important to think about **nutrition** when we choose which foods to eat.
   a construction   b food that keeps us healthy

9 Cooking the meat helped to **preserve** it, and so it stayed fresh longer.
   a keep from decaying   b position carefully

10 Firefighters' helmets provide **protection** against falling objects as well as heat.
   a warmth   b something that keeps you safe

2 **Adapt each of the sentences above to make a true statement about something you know or to make a sentence that is true for you.**

LISTENING 1   The discovery of fire

Before you listen

Do you know when fire was first used? How did this change people's lives? Discuss with a partner.

Global listening

🔊 **1.16 Listen to the presentation about the discovery of fire and answer the questions.**

1 What does the speaker mean by 'controlled use of fire'?
2 What four ways did fire impact daily life?
3 Which of these was a major turning point for people? Why?
4 How was the use of fire an application of technology?

> **THINK ABOUT:**
> food
> heat
> leisure activities & socializing
> light
> what they made
> where they lived

Close listening

LISTENING FOR CUES TO DISTINGUISH FACTS AND OPINIONS

In a presentation some ideas you hear are based on facts (i.e. something known to be true): *People use fire for cooking. We know that …*

Some are based on opinions (personal beliefs or ideas).

The fire <u>seems</u> dangerous. <u>It's hard to imagine</u> life without fire. That <u>looks</u> better.

Pay attention to the words a speaker uses to introduce an idea. This will help you to decide which ideas are facts and which are the opinions of the speaker.

🔊 1.16 **Listen to the presentation again. Decide if each sentence expresses a fact (*F*) or an opinion (*O*) based on the presentation. Compare with a partner.**

1 Fire was first used between 300,000 and 400,000 years ago.
2 The use of fire dramatically changed people's lives.
3 People were less afraid at night when they burned fires.
4 Cooking food allowed people to digest more nutrients and calories.
5 One benefit from cooking food was that it was easier to chew.
6 Cooking food allowed it to be preserved for longer.
7 When people had more food choices, they survived longer.
8 People's lives were better when they could socialize at night.
9 Cooking food doesn't seem like an application of technology.

Developing critical thinking

Discuss these questions in a group.

1 What would a world without fire look like? Think of what would be different in the world around us.
2 A current trend is to eat raw foods. What are the pros and cons of eating raw food?

ACADEMIC KEYWORDS		
application	(n)	/ˌæplɪˈkeɪʃ(ə)n/
fundamental	(adj)	/ˌfʌndəˈment(ə)l/
theory	(n)	/ˈθɪəri/

USEFUL LANGUAGE	
equipment	heat
food	transport

USEFUL LANGUAGE	
digestion	taste
energy	nutrition
health	weight

LISTENING 2 Forest fires: friend or foe?

Before you listen

Discuss the questions with a partner.

1 In what ways is a fire a 'foe' (enemy)?

2 In what ways might a fire be a 'friend'?

Global listening

 1.17 **Listen to the report on forest fires and check (✓) the topics mentioned.**

1 The main reason a forest fire is called a 'foe'. _____

2 A scientific description of what a fire needs to burn. _____

3 How a forest fire gets started. _____

4 The usual response to a forest fire. _____

5 Why the typical response is appropriate. _____

6 Why the typical response is inappropriate. _____

7 Several benefits of a forest fire. _____

8 The reasons why some trees plants and insects survive in areas where forest fires are common. _____

Close listening

> **LISTENING TO UNDERSTAND A SEQUENCE OF EVENTS**
>
> A sequence is a series of events that happen in order and lead to a result. To follow a sequence, listen for words and expressions that will tell you the order from the first event to the last event, such as: *first, second, third, then, next later, after that, after ... happens, then ..., afterward, eventually, finally, last.*
>
> Sometimes, a speaker doesn't present events in the order they happened. Therefore, it is important to use these signal words to help you keep track of the correct sequence.

1 1.17 **Listen again and decide if the sequence described in the sentences is correct or incorrect.**

1 If someone drops a burning match, a fire quickly burns out of control and then spreads.

2 A fire clears away dead trees and plants on the floor of the forest, then new plants can grow.

3 When the banksia bush grows, its seeds are released. When the fire starts, its cones are scorched.

4 After a fire starts, the blue beetle senses the fire, flies into the burning area, and lays its eggs while the fire is burning. Eventually the eggs are burned by fire in the trees.

5 After a fire, the ecosystem is restored because first the fast-growing plants start to grow, then the trees and finally the slower-growing plants.

2 **Work with a partner to make the sequence correct and add any other details you can remember.**

ACADEMIC KEYWORDS		
adapt	(v)	/ə'dæpt/
condition	(n)	/kən'dɪʃ(ə)n/
impact	(n)	/'ɪm,pækt/

Developing critical thinking

1 Discuss these questions in a group.

1 Should forest fires be put out quickly or allowed to burn? Discuss the pros and cons.

2 What are possible long-term benefits to an area of other natural disasters?

2 Think about the ideas from *The discovery of fire* and *Forest fires: friend or foe?* and discuss these questions in a group.

1 How important a role does fire play in daily life?

2 How does controlling fire and its uses help us to build and preserve communities?

USEFUL LANGUAGE

dangers	regeneration
ecosystem	soil
habitats	plant and
loss of life	animal life
nutrients	

Vocabulary skill

SYNONYMS

Synonyms are two or more words that have the same or almost the same meaning. There is often a slight difference in meaning so use a dictionary to check the usage and make a note of any differences, e.g. If one word is more formal or which words it can collocate with. Keep a list of synonyms.

For example:

extinguish / put out (informal)   *link / tie*

absolute / complete / total   *raw / uncooked*

Sometimes, we can also replace a word by a phrase or expression, especially in idiomatic speech. Some informal expressions based on 'fire' are:

to get burned   *to be on fire*   *to burn someone up*

to be fired up about something   *to be burned out*

1 Read each sentence. Circle two synonyms of the word in bold.

1 The controlled use of fire was a **turning point** in human history.
   a milestone   **b** pivotal moment   **c** extension

2 The controlled use of fire **dramatically** changed daily life in so
   many ways.
   a slightly   **b** substantially   **c** noticeably

3 One of the **fundamental** changes was in the way people ate.
   a essential   **b** key   **c** secondary

4 The impact on food choices was **significant**.
   a major   **b** meager   **c** considerable

5 It's hard to say if the destruction from a forest fire **outweighs** the
   benefit.
   a exceeds   **b** surpasses   **c** reduces

6 After the rain, the sun came out, and new plants **emerged** from the
   ground.
   a declined   **b** surfaced   **c** appeared

2 Read each sentence. Choose a synonym of the phrase in bold from the box and match it to the correct sentence.

doing great   excited   exhausted
makes me very angry   was cheated

1 I **got burned** at the market. I thought I'd bought designer jeans, but
   realized later they were fake. _____

2 He always keeps me waiting when we go out. That **burns me up**!
   _____

3 He's really **fired up** about playing the match on Saturday.
   _____

4 Yousef is **on fire:** he got the highest grade on the exam, and then he
   took first place at the sports meet. _____

5 Are you **burned out?** Find out about the symptoms of over-work and
   stress. _____

SPEAKING Debate: Does fire do more harm than good?

You are going to practice using stance markers, intonation to express feelings and attitudes, and changing a conversation topic and returning to it. You are then going to use these to have a debate.

Grammar

USING STANCE MARKERS

Stance markers are used by speakers to express their attitude about ideas they are presenting. They help us know if an idea is an opinion or a fact. Some ways to we can express stance are:

- with a single adverb.

Frankly, that sounds like a huge benefit.

Actually, being able to cook food was a major turning point for our ancestors.

- with adverbial clauses and prepositional phrases. In order not to sound impolite, try to support your stance with facts and relevant information.

As a matter of fact, I didn't do the project alone. Amid helped me.

To put it bluntly, I totally disagree with that idea. Let me explain why …

To be honest, that isn't really an example of how fire helps us. Consider this example …

1 🔊 1.18 **Listen. For each conversation, choose an appropriate response.**

1 **a** Frankly, it's too dangerous. **b** Actually, it's my favorite thing.

2 **a** Yeah, luckily it was late at night. No one was there. **b** Actually, it's next week.

3 **a** To be blunt, I thought it was boring. **b** Frankly, I'm not interested.

4 **a** To be honest, I can't. My friend did it. **b** Actually, I can't go. I'm busy.

2 **Complete the conversations with a stance marker. More than one choice is possible. Practice with a partner.**

1 **A:** That was an excellent restaurant. I'd definitely go there again.

    B: _____, I didn't like it at all. The service was awful.

2 **A:** You did great on the exam. You must have studied all weekend for it.

    B: _____, I spent over three weeks preparing for it. I knew it would be difficult.

3 **A:** I was worried I wouldn't be able to use this software, but _____, it's very easy to use.

    B: Yeah, I didn't have any problems with it either.

4 **A:** _____, I don't think we should go away for the whole weekend. We have a big project due next week, remember?

    B: Well, then how about just going out for one of the days?

Speaking skill

CHANGING THE TOPIC AND RETURNING TO IT

Sometimes in a conversation, you may want to change the topic briefly. This often happens when someone says something that reminds you of something else.

<u>Changing topic</u>

Sorry, that reminds me. Oh, by the way, Speaking of …,

Oh, before I forget, I want to mention …

<u>Returning to the topic</u>

Back to what we were talking about … Let's get back to … Anyway, …

As I was saying before, …

During a debate in which you have limited time to present your ideas, try only to go off the main debate topic briefly, and then quickly return to it.

1 ◖)) 1.19 **Listen to somebody describing an article. Which expressions from the box above do you hear?**

2 **Work with a partner to discuss the topics. Practice going off the topic briefly and returning to it.**

   1 The two most important possessions you would take if you needed to escape from a fire.
   2 A movie or TV show, or a book in which fire was a factor.

Pronunciation

USING INTONATION TO EXPRESS FEELINGS AND ATTITUDES

For someone to understand your ideas, they need not only to understand the words, but the feeling behind them. How quickly you say something, how your voice rises and falls, the tone and the pitch, all communicate your feelings and attitudes. By paying attention to your own intonation, you will make it easier for others to understand the ideas you want to communicate.

1 ◖)) 1.20 **Listen to the same sentence said with three different intonations. Match the emotion to the sentence.**

   1 I heard about a forest fire that happened recently. ___   a excited
   2 I heard about a forest fire that happened recently. ___   b afraid
   3 I heard about a forest fire that happened recently. ___   c uninterested

2 **Read each conversation. Decide what intonation will best communicate the ideas. Practice with a partner.**

   1 **A:** There was a big fire not far from here yesterday.
      B: I know. I was totally scared it was going to spread this way.
      A: No kidding! We were lucky they were able to put it out so quickly.
   2 **A:** Do you want to hear some absolutely wonderful news?
      B: Sure, what happened? Tell me!
      A: I got accepted to the school I was hoping to go to. I start next month!
   3 **A:** Hey, I'm not up for watching this movie.
      B: Me neither. It's pretty boring.
      A: Let's do something else.

SPEAKING TASK

For your debate, each side will present their ideas. Then you will have time to challenge the other side with questions.

Audience: classmates
Context: informal debate
Purpose: exchange and compare ideas in a structured format

BRAINSTORM

Work in a group of four. Discuss the many ways fire is part of life. Think about:

art   business   construction   manufacturing
medical treatment   natural world   recreation   travel

PLAN

1 Divide your group into two pairs.
   Pair 1: Present the ways the use of fire enhances our lives.
   Pair 2: Present the ways fire harms us.

2 Each pair makes a list of at least four ideas you plan to cover.
   Pair 1: Try to include a wide a range of the many ways in which fire benefits life.
   Pair 2: Consider including fires in natural disasters following earthquakes and volcanic eruptions.

For each idea on your list, discuss with your partner the details you want to include. Take notes. Then decide who will present each idea in the debate. Consider the stance markers and what tone of voice will best express your feelings and attitudes. Review the phrases to use to go off topic and return to the topic.

Debate ideas	Details to present

SPEAK

Work in the same groups as for exercise 1. Hold your debate. After each side presents, allow time for questions. Take brief notes on the other side's ideas.

SHARE

Work as a class to discuss the results of the debates. Choose one member of your group to summarize the main points presented in your debate. Compare ideas.

STUDY SKILLS Reviewing notes

Getting started

Discuss these questions with a partner.

1 Why is it important to review notes?
2 Do you review notes with classmates or alone?
3 What do you do when your notes are unclear or incomplete?

Scenario

Read this scenario and think about what Aida is doing right and what she is doing wrong to review her notes.

Aida is a busy second-year student. She attends six lectures a week. She has many pages to read in her textbooks every night. Every night at home she quickly reads over her notes. On the weekends she studies alone. Sometimes, she goes to the library where she reviews her notes by herself. If she sees a note that is unclear she writes *?* next to it, but she doesn't usually take time to ask someone for help or to look up the information in her textbook. Before exams, she goes over her notes, but her notes often aren't clear enough to help her prepare well for her exams. She often doesn't do as well on her exams as she would like to.

Consider it

Look at these suggestions for reviewing notes. With a partner discuss the advantages of each.

1 Read through your notes. Write ? next to anything that is unclear.
2 After the lecture check your textbook to find details missing from your notes.
3 Find a classmate to review notes together. Use your notes to discuss the main ideas of the lecture. Help each other to understand parts that are unclear to either of you.
4 Add to your notes or make corrections as you review them.
5 Ask yourself what do I understand? What do I need to get more information about?
6 Rewrite your notes to make them clear to you later, and to help you recall the information that you have reviewed.

Over to you

Discuss these questions with a partner.

1 Which of the pieces of advice do you already do?
2 Which ways of reviewing do you think are the most useful?
3 What advice would you give Aida on reviewing her notes?

Movement

LISTENING	Listening for similarities and differences
	Listening for supporting statements
VOCABULARY	Words with several uses
SPEAKING	Interrupting politely
PRONUNCIATION	Syllable stress and meaning

Discussion point

Discuss these questions with a partner.

1　Make a list of places you have lived or visited in your life. How far apart are these places?

2　Make a list of things you've bought recently. Do you know where they were made, produced, or grown? Which thing traveled the longest (or shortest) distance to reach you?

3　What are some products that are better when they are produced near you? What are some products that are better when they come from another place?

Vocabulary preview

1 Complete the sentences with a word from the box.

global	migrants	route	rural	trade	urbanization

1 I'd like to work for a _____ company with offices all over the world.

2 Because of _____, the cities in my country are growing rapidly.

3 I take the same _____ to school every day. I never take a different street.

4 Because of international _____, I own a lot of things that are made in China.

5 This town has a lot of _____ who have moved here from other parts of the world.

6 People who live in _____ areas in my country are usually farmers.

2 Do you agree with the sentences in exercise 1? Discuss them with a partner. Change the sentences if necessary to make them true for you.

LISTENING 1 Globalization in history

Before you listen

1 Work in groups. Look at the list of places. What do you think people in these places typically eat, drink, and produce? Use the items in the box or your own ideas.

chili peppers	electronics	potatoes	sugar	chocolate
oil	rubber	tea	coffee	porcelain	silk	tomatoes

1 China
2 Italy
3 Mexico

4 Saudi Arabia
5 the UK
6 the United States

2 Discuss where you think the items in exercise 1 came from originally.

Global listening

LISTENING FOR SIMILARITIES AND DIFFERENCES

In your academic work, you will often need to compare and contrast two or more ideas, places, people, or experiences. As you listen to lectures and other sources of information, it is important to actively ask yourself, 'How are these things similar? How are they different?'

You can also listen for expressions such as *Unlike X, …, Like X, …, Another similarity/difference is …* and comparative forms (*faster, a wider range of …*).

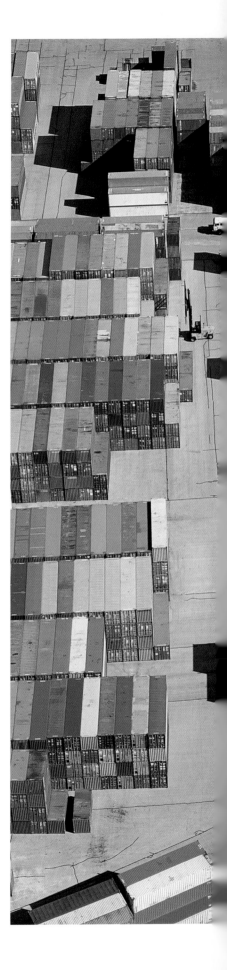

🔊 1.21 **Listen to the lecture on global trade networks in history. How are they similar or different? Check (✓) the network (or networks) that each sentence describes.**

	The Silk Road	The Columbian Exchange	Today's trade network
1 It is/was a global network.			
2 It is/was mostly controlled by the Middle East.			
3 Most goods are/were shipped by sea.			
4 China's main export is/was silk.			
5 It has/had an effect on cuisines and cultures.			

Close listening

🔊 1.21 **Listen to the lecture again. Where did these goods originally come from? Match the item with the place.**

1	tomatoes	___	a	China
2	coffee	___	b	Ethiopia and Yemen
3	silk	___	c	Brazil
4	black pepper	___	d	Mexico
5	potatoes	___	e	Peru
6	corn	___	f	South America and Mexico
7	chili peppers	___	g	India
8	rubber	___	h	South America

ACADEMIC KEYWORDS

adopt	(v)	/əˈdɑpt/
network	(n)	/ˈnetˌwɜrk/
significant	(adj)	/sɪɡˈnɪfɪkənt/

Developing critical thinking

Discuss these questions in a group.

1   Look at the goods in the close listening exercise above. Which of these goods does your country import? Which does it export? What else does your country often import or export?
2   How do you think globalization is affecting how people eat and drink in your country? Make a list of positive and negative changes.

USEFUL LANGUAGE
brands
chains
different cuisines
fast food
foreign food/restaurants
positive/negative change

LISTENING 2 Urbanization

ACADEMIC KEYWORDS

illustrate	(v)	/ˈɪləˌstreɪt/
rate	(n)	/reɪt/
statistics	(n)	/stəˈtɪstɪks/

Before you listen

Work in groups. You are going to hear a lecture on urbanization. How do you think the growth of cities will affect the areas below? Will the effects be positive or negative?

- families
- the economy
- health
- population growth
- crime
- rural life

Global listening

1 🔊 **1.22 Listen to the lecture from a political science course on urbanization. Circle the correct answers.**

1 Why are so many people moving from the countryside to the city?
   a Because there is a lot of poverty in rural villages.
   b Because many beautiful rural areas are disappearing.

2 Why does the professor think urbanization is mostly positive?
   a Because the number of migrants is increasing.
   b Because it has lifted millions of people out of poverty.

3 Why does the professor think urbanization will help the environment?
   a Because migrants send money back to rural areas.
   b Because the world's population will decrease in the future.

2 **What words or phrases from the lecture helped you find the answers?**

Close listening

LISTENING FOR SUPPORTING STATEMENTS

A supporting statement gives additional information, facts, or reasons for an idea or opinion. It is important to listen for supporting statements and the information they give, as this will help you understand the main ideas better. In spoken English, supporting statements usually come after a person gives an idea or opinion. However, many statements that come after an idea or opinion are *not* supporting statements. It is important to listen actively and identify the statements that actually give more information about an idea.

1 🔊 1.23 **Listen to the excerpts from the lecture. Check (✓) the information you hear. You may need to check more than one answer.**

1 'Some scholars say this movement from rural to urban is the biggest migration in human history.'
- a ☐ This is a big claim.
- b ☐ The world's population will increase by three billion people.
- c ☐ Billions of people will move to cities in the 21st century.
- d ☐ About 70% of the world's people will live in cities by 2050.

2 'Urbanization is happening very quickly and dramatically.'
- a ☐ In 1950, 86 million people lived in cities.
- b ☐ The number of cities with over a million people has gone from 86 to 400.
- c ☐ A lot of electronics are made in Shenzhen.
- d ☐ Shenzhen's population has increased from 25,000 to over 14 million.

3 'Life in a rural village is not easy.'
- a ☐ Rural areas in Asia and Africa can seem very beautiful to us.
- b ☐ Three quarters of people who earn less than a dollar a day are small farmers.
- c ☐ A dollar a day isn't very much money.
- d ☐ People in rural villages aren't as healthy and live shorter lives.

2 🔊 1.23 **Listen again. Discuss with a partner whether the information you checked in exercise 1 supports the main idea in each excerpt.**

Developing critical thinking

1 **Discuss these questions in a group.**
1 In the lecture, the professor believes that urbanization is mostly positive. Do you agree?
2 Is there a big city you'd like to move to? Why? What would you do there?

2 **Think about the ideas from *Globalization in history* and *Urbanization* and discuss these questions in a group.**
1 Look at the items in the list below. Which are effects of global trade? Which are effects of urbanization? Which are both? Can you think of more effects of global trade or urbanization?
- more foreign goods are available
- people learn more about other countries
- people have smaller families
- more energy is consumed
- people's ideas and values change
- more money goes to rural areas around the world
- factories close in some countries and open in others
- more people need to learn a second language
2 How can urbanization be a cause of increased global trade? How can global trade be a cause of urbanization?

THINK ABOUT:
crime
education
opportunities
population growth
poverty
the economy

Vocabulary skill

WORDS WITH SEVERAL USES

Many English words have more than one use, which can make listening comprehension quite difficult. For this reason, when you encounter a new word, or a familiar word used in a new way, it is useful to check for additional uses or meanings in a dictionary.

*When you think of traditional Italian cuisine, what comes to **mind**?* (mind = your attention or thoughts)

*These people can **mind** your kids while you're working.* (mind = look after someone for a short time)

*Would you **mind** turning off the TV? I'm trying to study.* (mind = feel annoyed)

1 🔊 1.24 **Complete the sentences from *Globalization in history* and *Urbanization* with the correct form of a word in the box. Then listen and check.**

adopt	export	good	illustrate
issue	network	produce	ship

1 Much later, Italians _____ the custom.

2 One of the first significant trade _____ was the Silk Road.

3 A lot of _____ were traded along the Silk Road.

4 For thousands of years, silk and porcelain were China's most important _____.

5 These trade routes developed after Christopher Columbus's _____ landed in the Americas in 1492.

6 Much of the _____ you see in the supermarket today was originally from the Americas.

7 Let me just give you some statistics to _____ this point.

8 That is great news for the environment, for global warming, and for a number of other _____ we face in the future.

2 🔊 1.25 **Now complete these sentences with the correct form of the same words from exercise 1. Then listen and check.**

1 Even today, almost 90% of the world's cargo is still _____ by sea.

2 Instead of silk, China _____ and _____ clothing, electronics, and more.

3 These places can be crowded, dirty, and sometimes dangerous, but they also do a lot of _____ for people.

4 The slum is where your _____ is. People from your village are already there.

5 The children's book was _____ with some very beautiful drawings.

6 Many people who cannot have their own children will _____ a baby.

7 There's an excellent article on urbanization in the new _____ of *Time*.

3 **Work in groups. Discuss how the meaning of each word is different in exercises 1 and 2. Use a dictionary to help you, if necessary.**

SPEAKING Giving a presentation about a city

You are going to learn how to use embedded questions to ask for information and to express what you do or do not know, how to interrupt politely, and how syllable stress affects a word's meaning. You are then going to use these skills to describe a global city.

Grammar

NOUN CLAUSES: EMBEDDED QUESTIONS

We can use embedded questions to ask a question more politely or indirectly, or to talk about what someone knows or remembers.

- Embedded questions begin with expressions such as *Can you tell me …?*
  Do you know …? and *I was wondering …*

  Do you know *where these things* **are** *from originally?* (= Where are they from originally?)

- They use sentence word order.

  I was wondering why *so many people* **move** *to cities.* (= Why do so many people move to cities?)

- In embedded questions with *be*, the verb changes position.

- In *yes/no* embedded questions, we use *if* or *whether* in place of a question word.

  Peter wants to know whether *there* **is** *one main cause of urbanization.*
  (= Is there one main cause of urbanization?)

1 Write embedded questions. Use the questions and the expressions in parentheses.

  1 Where were you born?   (*Can you tell me …?*)
  2 Did you grow up in the countryside?   (*I was wondering …*)
  3 What's your favorite kind of foreign food?   (*I'd like to know …*)
  4 Are you interested in living in another city or country?   (*Can you tell me …*)
  5 Are you going to move anywhere in the next year?   (*Do you know …?*)
  6 Have you ever tried food from an unusual place?   (*Can you tell me …?*)

2 Work with a partner. Ask and answer the questions in exercise 1.

Pronunciation skill

SYLLABLE STRESS AND MEANING

In some English words, the meaning of the word or its part of speech changes depending on which syllable is stressed.

For thousands of years, silk and porcelain were China's most important **exports**. (**EX**ports = noun)

Instead of silk, China produces and **exports** *clothing, electronics, and more.* (ex**PORTS** = verb)

Much of the **produce** *you see in the supermarket today was originally from the Americas.* (**PRO**duce (i.e. fruits and vegetables) = noun)

Instead of silk, China **produces** *and exports clothing, electronics, and more.* (pro**DUCE** (i.e. make) = verb)

1 🔊 1.26 Listen and repeat the example sentences in the box above.

2 🔊 1.27 **Listen to the sentences. Underline the stressed syllables in the words in bold. Then listen again and repeat. How does the meaning change?**

1   European countries **imported** silk from China.
2   Chinese silk was still a key European **import**.
3   Thanks to increased trade, there has been a **decrease** in the unemployment rate.
4   In 2050 the world's population will actually start to **decrease**.
5   The city's population is still **increasing**.
6   She earns $500 a week in the city. That's a huge **increase** from her job in the village.
7   Economists **project** that the trade deficit will continue to increase this year.
8   The transportation **project** is going to improve the lives of thousands.
9   He signed a **contract** to work in the London office for two years.
10 The economy has stopped growing and may now be **contracting**.

3   Work with a partner. Say five sentences describing your country with the words in exercises 1 and 2.

Speaking skill

INTERRUPTING POLITELY

In order to understand a lecture or classroom discussion clearly, it is sometimes necessary to interrupt and ask questions. In class, use more formal language and, if possible, try to signal before interrupting by raising your hand.

I'm sorry to interrupt. I was just wondering …

Excuse me for interrupting. Could I ask …

In class and in conversation, people also use words like *um, and, so,* and *but* to show that they would like to speak and get the other person's attention. To allow another person to interrupt you, you can say *Yes?* or *Go ahead.* If you don't want to be interrupted you can say *Sorry, let me finish.*

1   Complete the conversations with the expressions in the boxes. Then practice the conversations with a partner.

1

| I'm sorry | I was wondering | yes | OK |

A: … So that's a brief overview of urbanization in India. _____?
B: Oh, _____ to interrupt.
A: It's _____. Go ahead.
B: Well, _____ if this will be on next week's test.

2

| Can I ask | Excuse me. | Go ahead. |

A: I had a great week. On Monday, I attended a fascinating lecture, and on Wednesday —
B: Uh. _____
A: Yes? _____
B: _____ what the lecture was about?

2   Work with a partner. Choose a topic and tell your partner about it. Your partner interrupts and asks at least two questions. Then switch roles.

POSSIBLE TOPICS:

public transportation where you live

traffic where you live

a vacation that went badly

SPEAKING TASK

In pairs, present a global city.

Audience: classmates/peers

Context: an academic presentation and Q&A

Purpose: to describe a city and its connection to global systems

BRAINSTORM

Work with a partner. Make a list of cities you know that are 'global'. (These are cities where you can find people and products from all over the world.) What do you know about the cities in your list?

London

Dubai

Paris

Hong Kong

PLAN

1 🔊 1.28 Listen to two people give a presentation on a global city. Who are they presenting to and why?

2 🔊 1.28 Listen again. What information do they know? Check (✓) the questions that they are able to answer.
   1 ☐ How big is the city?
   2 ☐ Where are migrants to the city coming from?
   3 ☐ Why do people want to move to this city?
   4 ☐ What kinds of cuisine can you find in the city?
   5 ☐ What kind of work do people do there?
   6 ☐ What does the city (or the country it's in) produce?
   7 ☐ What are some places (cities or countries) it trades with?

3 Work with a partner. Choose a global city from your list (or another town or city you know well) and prepare a presentation about it. To prepare, first discuss the questions in exercise 1. Add any other interesting information you know about the city.

SPEAK

Give your presentation to two other pairs. Listen to the other pairs' presentations and politely interrupt to ask questions or add information.

SHARE

Find a new partner. Tell him or her about one of the presentations you heard.

USEFUL LANGUAGE

community

finance

housing

industry

services

tourism

trading partners

urbanization

Motivated learning

by Stella Cottrell

Motivation and goal-setting

Your level of motivation will affect your success, especially in slow or difficult patches. It is likely that there will be times when you get bored, frustrated, or anxious. You may feel as though a piece of work is just too much effort, or that you are struggling with your studies. You may even feel like giving up altogether. You will need clear motivation to keep yourself going even through such tough times.

Set goals

Make tasks more manageable by breaking them down into mini-goals. Set yourself small, short-term goals so that you are able to have lots of small successes. In time these add up to greater achievements.

Celebrate successes

Set targets and deadlines which are easy to meet — increase your chances of success. When you achieve a short-term goal (such as two hours' reading), reward yourself (for example, by taking a half-hour's break). Give yourself bigger rewards for completing whole tasks, to encourage yourself next time.

Mark success

Note down your achievements and successes in your journal — it is important to identify what you do well, so that you can do it again! After a few months, look back on your early work. Give yourself credit for any improvements you have made.

Aim for higher peaks

When you have met one set of goals, push yourself a bit harder. Make your next set of goals a little more challenging.

Find support

Find someone who encourages you and makes you feel good about yourself. Talk to this person about your goals and ambitions.

Which aspects of being a student appear like 'threats' or 'problems' to you at the moment? How could these be seen as challenges and opportunities?

Keep setting yourself new goals and challenges

Disease

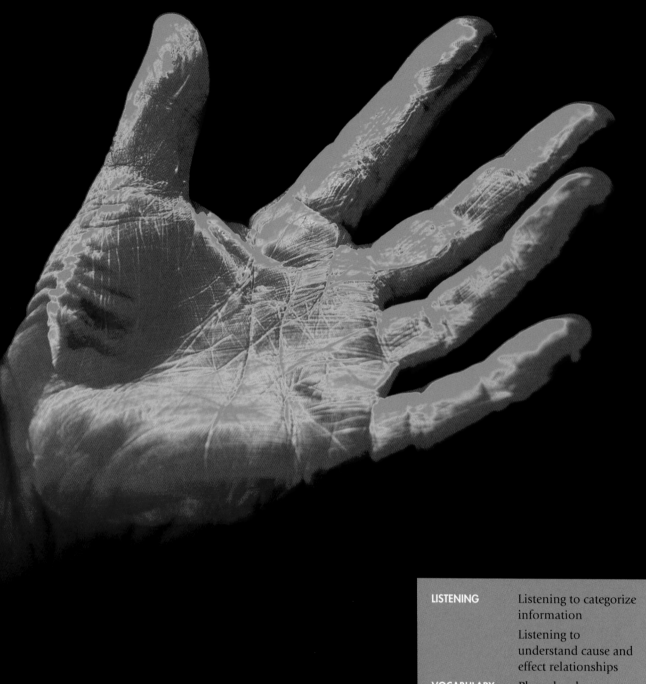

LISTENING	Listening to categorize information
	Listening to understand cause and effect relationships
VOCABULARY	Phrasal verbs
SPEAKING	Asking to clarify or confirm ideas you hear
PRONUNCIATION	Intonation with tag questions

Discussion point

Discuss these questions with a partner.

1 What kind of health problems are becoming more common in the 21st century? Which are becoming less common? Why?

2 What do you consider the main causes of diseases? Consider economics, lifestyle, and emotional wellbeing, as well as medical reasons.

3 What do you do to stay healthy?

Vocabulary preview

1 Read these sentences. In each set of five, match the words in bold with their meaning.

1 The heart **circulates** the blood through the lungs and out to the different parts of the body. ___

2 Until the 19ᵗʰ century most people believed in 'miasma theory' which **claimed** that diseases were caused by 'bad air'. ___

3 Both low and high **concentrations** of salt in the blood can be dangerous. ___

4 Experts estimate that the numbers of animals going **extinct** is between 1,000 and 10,000 times higher than is natural. ___

5 The **incidence** of infectious diseases often increases after a natural disaster. ___

a to say something is true (even though there is no proof)
b a large amount of something in a particular place
c the number of times something happens
d of something that no longer exists
e move round continuously (within a system)

6 Eye implants can **restore** perfect sight in blind patients. ___

7 There are **toxins** in apple pips and cherry stones that can make you ill. ___

8 All cases of bird flu have been **traced back** to direct contact with birds. ___

9 Bacteria and viruses that cause diseases can be **transmitted** in many ways, including by coughs and sneezes. ___

10 So far, there is no standardized and **valid** way to diagnosis 'burnout'. ___

f a poisonous substance
g to find the origin of something
h carry from one place to another
i reasonable and generally accepted
j to make something as good as it was before

2 Work with a partner. Decide if you think the statements in exercise 1 are true or false, and discuss anything else you know about these topics.

LISTENING 1 Germ myths

Before you listen

You will hear a radio show about germs and diseases. Work with a partner to answer the questions.

1 What are the main ways germs are spread?
2 In daily life, where are you likely to encounter germs?
3 If you have a cold, what do you do to keep from spreading it to others?

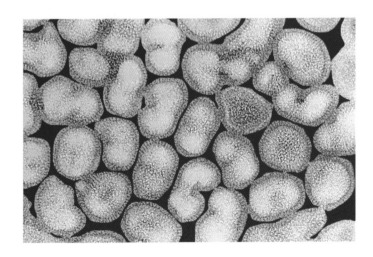

Global listening

LISTENING TO CATEGORIZE INFORMATION

In a presentation containing different categories of information, the speaker will often repeat certain key words to help you to follow the main ideas, and to guide you to which category each idea is in. After you finish listening, you can review the ideas in each category to help you to understand the main ideas of the presentation as a whole.

ACADEMIC KEYWORDS

claim	(v/n)	/kleɪm/
valid	(adj)	/'vælɪd/
vary	(v)	/'veri/

1 🔊 2.01 **Listen to a radio show about germs and disease. Complete the claims about germs.**

   1 Bacteria and viruses are the cause of _____.   True / Myth

   2 All germs are _____.   True / Myth

   3 Money is a major way that _____.   True / Myth

   4 The recirculating air on planes _____.   True / Myth

   5 Kitchens are _____.   True / Myth

   6 The 5-second rule says that _____.   True / Myth

2 **Decide if they are true or myths according to the show. Circle the correct answer in exercise 1.**

Close listening

🔊 2.01 **Read the sentences. Now listen again and complete the sentences.**

1 Dr. Mitchell says the common cold and influenza are caused by

   _____.

2 Some 'good' _____ in our bodies helps us to digest our food.

3 The amount of bacteria on a banknote depends on how _____ it is.

4 Dr. Mitchell thinks it is a _____ idea to wash our hands after touching money.

5 _____ airlines use air filters on airplanes.

6 If you get sick on a plane, it might be from the _____ next to you.

7 Dr. Mitchell says there are a lot of germs in a _____ cloth.

Developing critical thinking

Discuss these questions in a group.

1 Of the claims on the radio show, are there any you disagree with? Why?

2 How would you alter your behavior on a flight based on the report?

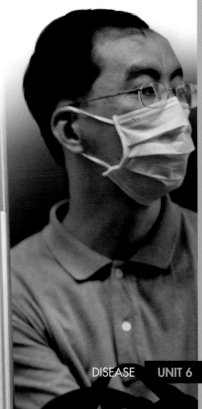

LISTENING 2 Disease detectives

Before you listen

1 Do you know what kind of habitats these animals live in? Do they live in water, or on land, or both? Categorize them. Add others you know.

prawn

snail

flying fox

dolphin	flying fox	frog	giraffe	hippo
prawn	snail	snake	tortoise	whale

2 What connection might there be between the animals in the photos and disease?

Global listening

1 🔊 2.02 **Listen to a lecture about diseases and answer the questions.**

  1 How many situations are described?
  2 Which countries did they take place in?
  3 What transmitted the diseases to humans in each case?

LISTENING TO UNDERSTAND CAUSE AND EFFECT RELATIONSHIPS

A speaker wants you to understand how ideas are connected, for example, how an action causes a result (or an effect). Here are some ways a speaker signals a cause and effect relationship:

*The high concentration of the toxin **caused** the disease.*

***The result was** the disease disappeared completely.*

Sometimes, the relationship is only implied (not stated):

There were no cases of the disease before the dam was built. (The dam caused it.)

When you take notes, you can use an arrow (→) to help you remember the cause and effect relationship:

went into river → sick

2 🔊 2.02 **Listen again. Then match sentence beginnings with the correct endings.**

  1 People in Senegal became ill _____
  2 The increase in snails led to _____
  3 The dam's destruction of the prawn's habitat _____
  4 Restoring the prawn habitat would result in _____
  5 Lytico-bodig seemed to be caused by _____
  6 Something caused more men _____
  7 When flying foxes became endangered, this _____
  8 Researchers figured out what caused _____

  a the diet of the Chamarro people.
  b the problem.
  c lytico-bodig to disappear in Guam.
  d than women to have the disease.
  e because of parasites in the water.
  f fewer snails and less disease.
  g caused the disease to decline.
  h more parasites being in the water.

Close listening

🔊 **2.02** **Listen again. Mark the sentences *T* (true) or *F* (false). Correct the false statements.**

1 There were only a few cases of the disease before the Diama Dam was built. ___
2 Most of the people had Schistosomaisis within two months of the dam being built. ___
3 When there were prawn to eat the snails, there was no Schistosomaisis there. ___
4 To solve the problem, researchers decided to kill the snails. ___
5 Researchers were correct that lytico-bodig was caused by the toxin in the seed. ___
6 Since men and women had the disease, both must have eaten some flying fox. ___
7 Disease caused the flying fox to disappear. ___
8 Researchers concluded that eating the flying fox probably caused the disease. ___

ACADEMIC KEYWORDS

cause	(n)	/kɔz/
investigation	(n)	/ɪn,vestɪ'geɪʃ(ə)n/
majority	(n)	/mə'dʒɔrəti/

Developing critical thinking

1 Discuss these questions in a group.

1 Do you think Project Crevette was a good long-term solution to the problem faced in Senegal? What might the pros and cons be of destroying a problem species vs. reintroducing a species that can control it naturally?
2 Think about what detectives do and what skills are involved. How might these be applied to understanding diseases? List your ideas. Then share with the class.

Activities and skills	Possible applications with diseases

THINK ABOUT:

changes to the environment
diet
location
living conditions
population movement
weather

2 Think about the ideas from *Germ myths* and *Disease detectives* and discuss these questions in a group.

1 What are the various factors that should be considered in order to understand the outbreak of a disease?
2 What are good ways to prevent the spread of a disease? Compile a list of ways and then rank them.

USEFUL LANGUAGE

cooking
diet
home environment
lifestyle
good sanitation
hand washing
quarantine
vaccination

Vocabulary skill

PHRASAL VERBS

A phrasal verb is made up of a verb + one or more particles (prepositions).
Since the meaning of a phrasal verb is different from the meaning of its
separate parts, you need to learn it as a different word. It can also be
useful to learn phrasal verbs as a lexical set related to a particular topic,
for example, to diseases and health.

*It is a myth that money is a major way you **pick up** diseases.*

*Say you **come down with** a cold after a flight, ...*

Note that some phrasal verbs are less formal than their one-word equivalents.

1 **Read the sentences. Match a synonym in the box to each phrasal verb in
bold related to health and disease.**

> catch   caught   cure   eliminated   prevent
> reduced   recovered from

1 My father **came down with** the flu and had to take a week off work.

   _____

2 Some say the best way to **get rid of** a cold is to just sleep a lot.

   _____

3 It's easier to **pick** germs **up** when you're traveling abroad.

   _____

4 My grandfather has **cut down on** his medicine from three pills to only
one. _____

5 After ten days, Aisha finally **got over** the virus and returned to class.

   _____

6 Drinking plenty of water can help **fight off** a cold. _____

7 I've **cut out** all snacks in order to try to lose weight. _____

2 **Work with a partner to answer the questions.**

1 What do you do or take if you
come down with a cold? How do
you fight it off?

2 If a friend wanted to lose weight,
what foods would you suggest
cutting down on or cutting out
altogether?

3 What would you recommend to
get rid of a headache?

4 Have you ever picked up germs
on a flight?

5 How long do you think it takes
to get over jet lag? Is there
anything you can do to avoid it?

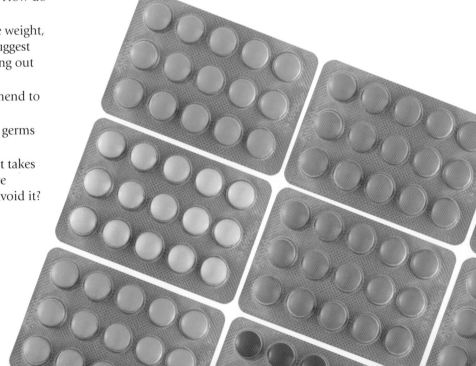

SPEAKING Discussion of research findings and applications

You are going to learn how to use modal auxiliaries in passive sentences, ways to clarify or confirm ideas you hear, and use the correct intonation with tag questions. You are then going to use these to discuss research findings and applications.

Grammar

USING MODAL AUXILIARIES IN PAST PASSIVE SENTENCES

Passive sentences are used when we want to put more emphasis on an action than on who or what did it. To speculate about *who* or *what* did the action, the passive voice with modal auxiliaries can be used.

Form	Example
May, *might*, and *could* indicate possibility based on some evidence.	The disease **may/might/could have been** spread by the water. (We don't know for sure.)
Must and *had to have* indicate a stronger possibility based on stronger evidence.	The disease **must have been** spread by the snails. (We know there was a big increase in snails.) The disease **had to have been** spread in the water. (Everyone who went in the water became ill.)
Can't is used to talk about certainty in a negative sentence.	It **can't have been** flu if you got better in three days. (I'm pretty sure it wasn't.)

1 **Read each situation. Then complete the sentences with a correct modal. In some cases, more than one choice is possible.**

1 A man with a headache took some medicine, and then he felt better.

The headache _____ cleared up by the medicine.

2 The town built a new medical clinic and put in a water purification facility. There was a decrease in illness.

The decrease in illness _____ caused by better care at the clinic, or it _____ due to having cleaner water.

3 My family all ate the same food last night but only my parents got sick.

The sickness _____ caused by the food since not everyone got sick.

4 A woman drank four cups of strong tea at a dinner with friends. She couldn't fall asleep that night.

The tea _____ keeping her awake.

5 Three children who drank from the same cup, and then played with the same toy became ill.

A virus _____ transmitted by the cup, or it _____ spread by the toy.

2 **Work in groups. Discuss possible explanations for these situations. Try to use past passive modals where you can.**

1 In many parts of the world, people are healthier and living longer than they were thirty years ago.

2 In the past twenty years, there has been a significant increase in childhood allergies worldwide.

3 People are now surviving diseases that they didn't in the past.

4 The incidence of obesity has been increasing worldwide.

Speaking skill

ASKING TO CLARIFY OR CONFIRM IDEAS YOU HEAR

To clarify an idea means to ask a question to make sure you have understood the idea clearly. To confirm an idea means that you restate in your own words what you understood, and then you ask if you understood the speaker correctly. These are both very useful strategies in discussions.

<u>To clarify an idea</u>

Do you mean …? What do you mean by …? Could you clarify … for me?

<u>To confirm an idea</u>

So you mean that …? I understood that … Is this correct?

So, your (main) point is …? You just explained why …, correct?

1 ◉ 2.03 **Listen to the conversation. Complete the questions.**

1 _____ by environmental factors?

2 _____ that disease is caused by stress?

3 _____ you think stress was the biggest factor?

2 **What is the speaker's opinion of the relationship between stress and disease? Do you agree?**

3 **Work in a group. Discuss the following questions. Give reasons to support your ideas. Clarify and confirm ideas you hear.**

1 What do you consider a healthy diet?

2 How important is fitness and exercise to preventing disease?

3 What are good ways to relax and reduce stress?

Pronunciation skill

INTONATION WITH TAG QUESTIONS

When we use tag questions such as *didn't they?* and *is it?* we use either rising or falling intonation, depending on the meaning we want to express.

We use rising intonation to ask a genuine question:

That hurts, doesn't it? (I'm not sure but it looks painful.)

We use falling intonation when we are already fairly sure of the answer:

That hurts, doesn't it? (I know it hurts because I've done the same thing!)

Falling intonation + heavy stress is used to express sarcasm:

That was a GREAT idea to build the dam, wasn't it? (**not** a good idea)

1 ◉ 2.04 **Complete the questions and mark the intonation. Then listen and check.**

1 **A:** Hey, this energy drink tastes great, _____?

   B: Yeah, it isn't too sweet, _____?

   A: Well, it is quite sweet, but I like sweet things!

2 **A:** The table looks dirty, _____?

   B: You're right. We should clean it off before we use it.

3 **A:** I'm afraid I lost my phone again.

   B: That was clever, _____? You've lost it four times now!

   A: Hey that's not fair! I've only lost it three times!

2 **Now practice the conversations with a partner.**

SPEAKING TASK

Work in a group to solve a medical mystery. Then present your findings to the class.

Audience: classmates

Context: classroom / public health

Purpose: analyze data, and then discuss conclusions regarding a medical mystery

BRAINSTORM

Imagine you are on a team whose task it is to solve a medical mystery. Read the situation.

A woman in London went to an airport to pick up her friend who was returning from a trip to Thailand. Her friend's flight was late. She decided to eat dinner and have a cup of tea while she waited for the flight. About a week later, the woman started to get sick. At first, she just had a headache, but then she developed a fever. She had chills and was also very tired. She went to the doctor, who said she had influenza.

She continued to get worse. Finally, after visiting several other doctors she was diagnosed with malaria. The woman couldn't understand how she could possibly have malaria, which is transmitted by mosquitoes. Over 100 countries worldwide have a risk for malaria, but not England. In addition, she hadn't traveled anywhere for a year.

PLAN

Think about possible explanations for how the woman might have developed malaria. Organize your ideas. Take notes on any details you want to include.

The malaria could have been spread by:	Notes and details

SPEAK

Work in a group. Take turns presenting your ideas. Clarify and confirm ideas you hear. Use tag questions to make sure you understand everything correctly. Decide together on the best explanation for why the woman came down with malaria.

SHARE

Have someone in your group present your group's explanation to the whole class. Compare ideas. Vote on the best explanation.

STUDY SKILLS Leading a group

Getting started

Discuss these questions with a partner.

1 What do you enjoy in group discussions?
2 What factors make a group discussion difficult to participate in?
3 What qualities are important in a group leader?

Scenario

Read this scenario and think about what Ahmed does right and what he does wrong to lead a group discussion.

Consider it

Look through these suggestions for being an effective group leader. Work with a partner to discuss why they are important.

1 Prepare for the discussion. Get organized on what the group will talk about.
2 Ask questions to start the discussion and to keep it going, but don't dominate the discussion.
3 Make sure everyone has a turn to speak and allow people to speak without interruptions.
4 Check that the group stays on topic, and guide the group to return to the topic, as needed.
5 Encourage everyone to ask questions and to confirm that they understood ideas correctly.
6 Ask someone to take notes on the discussion.
7 Have the group review the notes, and check that they represent the main ideas covered by the group.

Over to you

Discuss these questions with a partner.

1 Which of these suggestions do you or your classmates already do?
2 Which of these suggestions would you want to try?
3 What advice would you give Ahmed on leading a group?

Ahmed has been chosen to lead the study session. He hasn't done it before and he is nervous about being able to do a good job. Before the session, he makes a list of questions to talk about. At the beginning, he talks for a long time about his own ideas. Then, he asks the other members for their ideas. His classmates all start talking at once. He is excited because it seems as if they are having a lively discussion. Then, he notices one of his classmates hasn't said anything. He stops the discussion and asks that classmate a question. When a different classmate starts to answer, he tells him to let the first classmate answer without being interrupted. At the end, Ahmed wants to review the main ideas of their discussion, but realizes no one was taking notes.

Survival

LISTENING	Using prior knowledge to predict the content of a presentation
	Listening for structure signals that connect ideas
VOCABULARY	Learning word families after listening
SPEAKING	Contributing additional information to a discussion
PRONUNCIATION	Question intonation

Discussion point

Discuss these questions with a partner.

1   What should our priorities be to ensure our survival in the future?
2   What can we do to protect the natural world in the long term?
3   If a major storm was approaching where you live, where would you go and what would you do to protect yourself?

Vocabulary preview

Read each sentence. Then (circle) the definition closest in meaning to the word in bold. Compare with a partner.

1 It is important that the development of the world's wild places is controlled to **ensure** the survival of endangered species.

   a to do something to be certain of a result   **b** persuade someone

2 Recent **findings** suggest that marriage improves the life expectancy of men.

   a information learned from a study   **b** movements

3 The event was held to **foster** a spirit of cooperation between the two communities.

   a to oppose   **b** help to develop

4 It's often the people who have least who behave with the most **generosity** in an emergency situation.

   a beginning of something   **b** willingness to give time, money, etc.

5 We need to take care of the environment or we will **jeopardize** the ability of future generations to survive.

   a know about   **b** risk losing or damaging something valuable

6 It's surprising what kind of shelter can be built using only **limited** materials like some wood and a few stones.

   a not very great in amount   **b** easy to pull or bend

7 To be healthy, it's a good idea to **minimize** the amount of junk food we eat, and to **maximize** the amount fresh fruits and vegetables we consume.

   a make smaller/larger in degree   **b** to make louder/softer

8 The house plans were **modified** in order to include an extension for the grandparents to live in.

   a make changes to improve   **b** move quickly

9 Our family often helps our neighbors, and they often help us. This **reciprocity** builds a strong bond between us.

   a something unfamiliar   **b** something similar done for each other

10 We were **sustained** by letters of support during the difficult period.

   a reduced   **b** given strength and hope

LISTENING 1 Kindness as a survival skill

Before you listen

1 **What does it mean to be kind to someone? Rank the actions below from 1–5 (1 = most kind). Compare with a partner's ranking.**

   ____ Lend a friend some money.

   ____ Do an errand for an elderly neighbor or family member.

   ____ Donate to an international relief organization.

   ____ Help an injured stranger.

   ____ Give some flowers to someone who is ill.

USING PRIOR KNOWLEDGE TO PREDICT THE CONTENT OF A PRESENTATION

Use your own experiences and knowledge about a topic to predict what you are going to hear.

This will help you prepare for the listening and will get you thinking about the topics and issues that are likely to be covered. Use the title, any visuals, and read the questions to help you prepare.

---

2 Read the title of this listening section. How might kindness be a survival skill?

3 What kind acts do you think you might hear about? Share your ideas with a partner.

Global listening

1 ◉ 2.05 **Listen to the podcast and answer the questions.**

　1 Were any of the kind acts you listed mentioned?

　2 What are personal examples of the kind acts you heard mentioned?

2 Circle **the phrases that best complete the sentences.**

　1 The woman decided to leave extra money at the café because she was **very wealthy / concerned about her neighbors**.

　2 A man helps his neighbor fix his roof. The following week the neighbor helps him with his garden. This is an example of **direct / indirect** reciprocity.

　3 The coffee shop tale is about **direct / indirect** reciprocity because the people who gave money **expected / didn't expect** a specific person to help them out.

　4 The speaker believes people help after a natural disaster because we **expect direct reciprocity in the future / naturally help one another to survive**.

　5 The man who saved children from the river risked his life because he **wanted to be a hero / knew instinctively it was the right thing to do**.

Close listening

◉ 2.05 **Listen again and write T (true) or F (false). Then correct the false sentences.**

1 The woman was the only customer to leave money. ___

2 The speaker refers to bonds within families as well as with friends. ___

3 Examples of emergency aid mentioned are food, water, and housing. ___

4 The car in the river had three children in it. ___

5 By building bonds of reciprocity, trust develops. ___

6 The speaker concludes that building communities is essential for survival. ___

Developing critical thinking

Discuss these questions in a group.

1 What reasons does the speaker in the podcast give for why reciprocity is important? Which do you think is the most important?

2 Can you think of examples of direct and indirect reciprocity from your own lives or those of people you know of?

LISTENING 2 Building for the future

Before you listen

Everyone needs a place to live. One challenge for the 21ˢᵗ century is to design housing to meet a growing need. With a partner, discuss the issues that face contemporary architects and make a list.

Global listening

> **LISTENING FOR STRUCTURE SIGNALS THAT CONNECT IDEAS**
>
> A presentation may have several subtopics, which contribute information to help you to understand the main topic. At the beginning of the presentation, the speaker often presents the main topic and the subtopics so that you will know how the presentation is organized; for example:
>
> ***Today we're talking about*** *green building.* (main topic)
>
> ***We're going to focus on*** *energy use* (subtopic) *and building reuse* (subtopic)…
>
> To make a transition from one subtopic to the next, the speaker will often use phases such as: *regarding, as for, turning to, another important consideration.* Paying attention to these phrases will help you know when the speaker is moving from one subtopic to the next.

THINK ABOUT:

cost

demand

energy use

limited global resources

population increase

sustainability

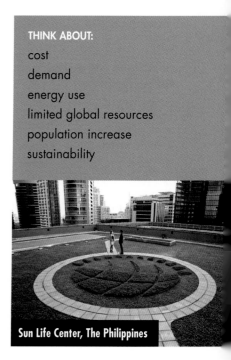

Sun Life Center, The Philippines

1 ◗) 2.06 **Read the phrases below. Listen to the lecture *Building for the future* and match each phrase to the subtopics it connects.**

    a Regarding the…   **b** Now let's look at…

    c With this in mind…   **d** Taking that into consideration…

    1 current challenge → the trend of 'green building'   ____

    2 overview of presentation → the principles of green building   ____

    3 principles of green building → energy use   ____

    4 new "green" construction → building reuse   ____

2 ◗) 2.06 **Listen again and complete the gapped summary with the words in the box. How many of the issues from your list were mentioned?**

> environmentally responsible   in the future
> it is used   new   use resources wisely

The building challenge we face is to meet the needs of people both now and
¹ _____ . Because there are limited resources, we need to
design buildings that ² _____ . The main goals of green
building are based on being ³ _____ both when a building
is constructed as well when ⁴ _____ . Reusing existing
buildings for ⁵ _____ purposes is also a good way to save
limited natural resources like wood and metal.

World Trade Center, Bahrain

Close listening

1 🔊 2.06 **Listen to the lecture again and complete the table using no more than three words in each gap.**

ACADEMIC KEYWORDS

content (n) /ˈkɑnˌtent/
emphasize (v) /ˈemfəˌsaɪz/
resources (n) /ˈriˌsɔrs/

Listening skills

Principles of green building	- building is 1) _____ - 2) _____ with surroundings - resource conservation - meets 3) _____ - better to 4) _____ an old building than 5) _____ a new one
Design considerations	- must be 6) _____ for the people who use it Germany: 7) _____ solar benefit - more 8) _____ for light and warmth in 9) _____ - trees for 10) _____ in summer Egypt: - 11) _____ strong sunlight during the day - trees to 12) _____ sunlight year round

2 **Complete the statements. Compare with a partner.**

1 Three renewable or recycled building materials mentioned are _____
2 Three renewable energy resources mentioned are _____
3 One reason given for why it is beneficial to use local materials is _____
4 The most important design feature of Masdar City is _____
5 The Sydney Olympics facilities became _____
6 The acquatic center in Beijing became _____
7 Namba parks was previously _____

Developing critical thinking

1 **Discuss these questions in a group.**

1 Using renewal resources such as solar, wind, and geothermal energy are all ways to meet energy needs. In which countries would each of these be good options to develop?
2 Namba Parks in Osaka, Japan, is a planned community where many people can live and work in a small area. What might the pros and cons of living in this type of community be?

Namba Parks, Japan

2 **Think about the ideas from *Kindness as a survival skill* and *Building for the future* and discuss these questions in a group.**

   1 If you were designing a building that used resources wisely and maximized opportunities for the people who used it to build a community, what would it look like?

   2 Providing shelter is a global challenge. What are ways countries can work together to make best use of limited resources to meet this challenge?

Vocabulary skill

LEARNING WORD FAMILIES AFTER LISTENING

When you learn a new vocabulary word, you can increase your vocabulary further by learning the other parts of speech related to the word.

generous	generosity		
survive	survivor	survival	
sustain	sustainer	sustainability	
recycle	recycler	recycling	recycled
modify	modification		

1 **Complete each group of sentences with the correct form of the word.**

   generous   generosity

   1 The family was very _____. Their _____ enabled the community to have enough money to build a sports complex.

   survive   survivor   survival

   2 After the accident there was only one _____. The doctors were amazed he was able to _____ for hours before help came.

   sustain   sustainer   sustainability

   3 As the world population increases, it will become more difficult for everyone. In fact, _____ has become a concern for many people.

   recycle   recycler   recycling   recycled

   4 Using _____ building materials is a good way to save limited resources. Unfortunately, it isn't always possible to _____ materials. However, the number of _____ companies is increasing as people world-wide become aware of the need to be environmentally responsible.

2 **Use a dictionary to find the other forms of the words below. Write them down. Work with a partner to say sentences using the forms of the words.**

   reciprocity   minimize   maximize

SPEAKING Group discussion on water issues

You are going to practice using present unreal conditionals, ways to contribute ideas to a discussion, and how to use intonation to communicate your ideas. You are then going to use these to have a group discussion on a global survival challenge: water.

Grammar

THE PRESENT UNREAL CONDITIONAL

You can use the present unreal conditional to talk about something that is imagined, impossible, or 'contrary to fact.' Note we use the past tense, although we are not talking about the past.

Form	Example
If clause (Past tense) + result clause (*would* + infinitive)	*If a stranger **saw** that my children needed help, he **would help** them*
With the verb *be*, use *were* for all subjects.	*If I **were** a disaster victim, **I'd be** grateful to receive help from others.* *If he **weren't** busy, he **would help** me.*
Might and *could* + base form can be used to express a possible result.	*If they **planted** trees, they **could keep** the building cooler.* *If they **used** more wood or bamboo, they **might reduce** their costs.*
Question forms are made by putting the words in the main clause in question word order.	*If you **had** the opportunity, **would** you **live** in a green building?*

1 **Make sentences using the present unreal conditional.**

1 The village is very poor. (money / build a well)
2 The neighbors don't help each other. (help / a stronger community)
3 The builders don't use local materials. (local materials / save resources)
4 The houses aren't strong enough to withstand the earthquake. (strong / people feel safer)
5 The windows are very small. (bigger / let in more light)

2 **Work in pairs. Complete and practice the first conversation. Then have similar conversations using the prompts below.**

1 **A:** Do you want to go out to a restaurant tonight?
   B: If I _____ so busy, I could. Unfortunately, I have homework to finish for tomorrow.
2 **A:** Let's [suggest possible activity] tonight.
   B: If I [problem you have now], I could. Unfortunately, …
3 **A:** If we _____ the time, we [suggest activity].
   B: Yeah, or we [suggest possible alternative].
4 **A:** If we were studying English in London, we [possible activity].
   B: Yeah, and we [other possible activity].

3 **Work in pairs. Take turns asking and answering the questions.**

1 If you had more free time, how would you spend it?
2 If you had three wishes, what would you wish for?
3 If you could travel anywhere, where would you go?
4 If you could meet an important person, who would it be?

Speaking skill

CONTRIBUTING ADDITIONAL INFORMATION TO A DISCUSSION

There are different ways you can contribute ideas to a discussion:

- your own knowledge: *As far as I know, ... As I understand it, ... What I've been told is ...*
- your own idea and opinions: *I feel that ... What I've found ... In my view ...*
- other information you have heard or read: *I recently read/heard that ... There was a recent story about ... I saw something on the Internet that said ...*

1 🔊 2.07 **Listen to the discussion. What do the students contribute? Mark the category in the chart. Then summarize the discussion with a partner.**

Student	Own knowledge	Own opinion	Other information
1			
2			
3			
4			

2 **Work in a group to review the main ideas from *Building for the future*. Contribute additional information to the discussion.**

THINK ABOUT:

additional examples
building material use and reuse
current and future needs
energy use
examples from *Building for the future*
principles of green buildings

Pronunciation skill

QUESTION INTONATION

The intonation you use lets others know if you are making a statement or asking a question.

<u>Use falling intonation</u>

- for *wh-* Qs: *Where would you like to live?*

- to indicate a choice between two things:

Do you want to use wood or stone for the house?

<u>Use rising intonation</u>

- for *Yes/No* questions: *Are you interested in green building design?*

- To change a statement to a question without changing the word order. This is often used to show surprise or shock:

You don't think saving energy is important? (That's hard to believe!)

1 🔊 2.08 **Listen to the sentences. Then listen again and repeat.**

1 Is the building design for a hotel or a school?
2 You would live in a house that re-used water from the washing machine?
3 In the design, do the windows face north or south?
4 She really gave away that much money?
5 Are you planning to do that by yourself?

2 **Work with a partner. Practice the conversations with correct intonation.**

1 **A:** Do you want me to help you move that furniture? It looks heavy.
   B: You would help me do that? That would be great.
2 **A:** I ran 20 kilometers yesterday at the park.
   B: You ran 20 kilometers? I could never do that.
3 **A:** Would you prefer to live in a warm climate or a cold climate?
   B: A warm climate. I wouldn't like cold winters.

SPEAKING TASK

Experts have said that water is one of the biggest survival challenges of the 21st century. Work in a group to discuss the global water challenge.

Audience: peers/classmates
Context: student presentation
Purpose: practice in synthesizing new ideas and applying to another context

BRAINSTORM

1   Read the information. What is the predicted situation for 2050?

> Seventy percent of the Earth is covered by water, but 97% of that water is salt water. Of the other 3%, only 1% is available for people to use. Global water consumption has quadrupled in the last 50 years, primarily due to increases in world population, along with increases in manufacturing in developing countries, and to more large-scale agricultural practices. By 2050, it is predicted that about a quarter of the world's population will have regular water shortages. This is a global sustainability issue.

2   Work in a group to answer these questions.

   1   What is water used for where you live?
   2   Is water an issue where you live?
   3   What are some ways communities can re-use water and use water efficiently in parks, landscaping, and public buildings?
   4   What are specific ways people can reduce water use at home?
   5   What are other ways of possibly getting access to water besides desalinization (removing salt from sea water), or taking advantage of melting ice caps?

PLAN

Work alone to organize your ideas on what you consider the best ways to use water efficiently and to meet the global water challenge.

Water

SPEAK

Review your ideas in your group. Compare ideas and opinions, and contribute additional ideas to the discussion. Use conditional sentences to discuss possible situations.

SHARE

Present your group's ideas to other classmates. Together, compile a list of ways people at home and in public can use water efficiently to meet the global challenge.

Independent study

by Stella Cottrell

Types of independent study

Independent study is a feature of all university programs. The amount and the kind varies from one program to another.

Negotiated independent study

You may be able to study all or part of your degree by negotiated independent study, designing your programs according to given learning outcomes. With this approach, you agree the relevant title, approach, outputs, and resources with your tutor. Although you have some ongoing contact with your tutor, there may not be any taught sessions.

Independent study within a degree program

In most programs, 'independent study' means working on your own between taught sessions. Early on you are given more guidance, though probably still less than you received at school or college. As you move through the program, you are usually given more choices and greater personal management of the study process. The amount of independent study increases until you write your dissertation, which you do almost completely by independent study.

Levels of independence

Different levels of independence are involved for each program and for each year. This depends on how far you:

- have control over the content, design, and learning outcomes for the module, unit, or degree
- study from resources rather than attend taught sessions
- have choices over modules or options
- decide the pace of study
- are expected to study on your own each week
- can choose where and when you study
- can choose your assignment titles
- can choose how you will be assessed.

Independent learning can be all the things you would *like* it to be! University learning allows you a great deal of freedom to shape your learning experience to suit yourself. The better your study skills, the easier you will find managing that freedom so that you can enjoy yourself while undertaking independent study successfully. It is up to you to manage that process well.

Activity

What does 'independent study' suggest to you?

1   In pencil, underline all the words below that you associate with the phrase 'independent study'.

freedom   making my own success

going it alone   failure!

less help

being in control   maturity

isolation

pursuing my own interests

good study management

free time

responsibility

less guidance

managing my time

being left to do what I want

working on my own   finding support

enjoyment

2   Using a bright marker pen, circle all the words that describe how you would *like* independent study to be. Use the bubbles to add words of your own.

Drive

Discussion point

Discuss these questions with a partner.

1 Think about what drives you in your life. Which of these do you think is most important: to be healthy, to be happy, or to be rich? Explain your opinion.

2 Which do you think drives people more, rewards or punishments? Why?

3 What are some goals you have for this year, for the next few years, and for your whole life?

Vocabulary preview

1 **Complete the survey with the words in the box.**

| hoard | motivation | physiological | possessions | respect | self-esteem |

WHAT DRIVES YOU?

Check (✓) the statements that describe you.

___ 1 I don't need fancy things. I only care about basic _____ needs like food and water.

___ 2 Money is my main _____ in life. That's the only reason why I work/study.

___ 3 I'm always ready to move or travel. I could fit all of my _____ in a couple of suitcases.

___ 4 A sense of belonging is important to me. I need the _____ of my classmates/colleagues to be happy.

___ 5 A big concern for me is safety. I _____ large quantities of food and water in case there's a disaster.

___ 6 I have good _____. I like myself the way I am, and I'm happy with my life currently.

2 **Now take the survey. Check (✓) the statements that are true for you. Then compare your ideas in groups. Which statements did people check most often?**

LISTENING 1 What makes some people hoarders?

Before you listen

1 **Make a list of the three most important things you own and answer the questions.**

1 How long have you had each thing?

2 Why do you have it?

3 Where do you keep it?

2 **Discuss these questions with a partner.**

1 Do you consider yourself a neat person or a messy person?

2 How do you keep things organized in your home?

3 Do you know anyone who has a very messy home?

4 What do you think drives some people to hoard things?

Global listening

))) 2.09 **Listen to a news report on hoarders. According to the expert, what do most hoarders have in common? Check (✓) the correct answers.**

1 They don't make decisions easily.   ____

2 They are perfectionists.   ____

3 They were poor in the past.   ____

4 They had difficult relationships with their parents. ____

<table>
<tr><td colspan="3">ACADEMIC KEYWORDS</td></tr>
<tr><td>assist</td><td>(v)</td><td>/ə'sɪst/</td></tr>
<tr><td>in common</td><td>(adj)</td><td>/ɪn 'kɑmən/</td></tr>
<tr><td>reduce</td><td>(v)</td><td>/rɪ'dus/</td></tr>
</table>

Close listening

▪ LISTENING TO UNDERSTAND VOCABULARY FROM CONTEXT ▪

When listening to lectures and other sources of information, you will often encounter new words. In these cases, you can often use the context to guess the word's meaning. You can ask yourself:

- How does the word relate to the topic or context? (e.g. *She is an administrator at a local school, where her desk is always neat and tidy. Administrator* is probably a kind of job people do in a school or office.)

- Do you know any other words that could also be used in this context? (e.g. *secretary, assistant, office worker*)

- Based on the context, what part of speech is this word?

- Does its meaning sound positive, negative, or neutral?

- Does the word sound formal or informal, academic or conversational, serious or humorous?

))) 2.10 **Listen to the excerpts from the news report. Listen for the words in bold and use the context to guess the meaning. Circle the best definition for each word.**

1	administrator	a	security guard	b security
2	stuff	a	crowded and untidy	b a variety of things
3	piles	a	a long distance	b objects one on top of another
4	junk	a	useful things	b useless things
5	strain	a	tension and pressure	b fun and pleasure
6	specializes	a	suffers from	b is an expert in
7	impair	a	hurt	b two things that don't match
8	traits	a	qualities	b differences
9	misconception	a	true fact	b false assumption
10	clutter	a	emptiness	b mess

Developing critical thinking

Discuss these questions in a group.

1 What advice would you give someone who has a hoarding problem?

2 Frederick Taylor describes several traits of hoarders. Which do you think is most important? What else might make someone a hoarder?

- Care about others
- Care about objects
- Difficulties making decisions
- Difficulties categorizing
- Perfectionists
- Fear of forgetting things
- Difficult relationships with parents, especially fathers

USEFUL LANGUAGE
ask for help
organize
seek professional help
set aside time to (do something)
set up a filing system
sort out
talk to someone
throw away

LISTENING 2 The hierarchy of needs

Before you listen

Work in groups. Discuss the questions below.

1 The things below are all essential to life. Which one is most important? Number them from 1 (most important) to 5 (least important).

___ air ___ food ___ shelter ___ sleep ___ water

2 Look at the list of things many people want to accomplish in their lives. How important are they to you? Add two accomplishments to the list, then number them from 1 (most important) to 5 (least important).

___ finish school ___ get married ___ find a good job

___ _____ ___ _____

3 Think of some well-known entertainers, athletes, businesspeople, artists, and philanthropists (people who give money to charity). What do you think motivates them?

Global listening

🔊 **2.11** **Listen to the lecture on Maslow's hierarchy of needs. What are the main categories of needs in Maslow's pyramid? Check (✓) the correct answers.**

- [ ] **a** physiological
- [ ] **b** financial
- [ ] **c** safety
- [ ] **d** love and belonging
- [ ] **e** environmental
- [ ] **f** self-esteem
- [ ] **g** self-actualization
- [ ] **h** artistic

Close listening

LISTENING FOR NOTE TAKING

Listening to a class lecture is different from listening to news reports or other sources because you will need to record important information for tests, essays, and more. For this reason, it is important to decide which information to include in your notes. In addition to writing down main ideas, topics, and information on the board, it is also important to listen for cues from the professor about which information is important.

1 🔊 **2.11** **Listen to the lecture again. Complete the notes with the information you hear.**

ACADEMIC KEYWORDS		
propose	(v)	/prəˈpoʊz/
tier	(n)	/tɪr/
vital	(adj)	/ˈvaɪt(ə)l/

Maslow's hierarchy

Remember: needs are ranked; it's a ¹ *hierarchy* _____ of needs

Self-actualization
be the best you can be

Self-esteem
⁵ _____ from others and for yourself

Love and belonging
family friends ⁴ _____

Safety
physical safety possessions ³ _____

Physiological
air ² _____ water sleep shelter

Important: Not everyone agrees with Maslow ... his theory does not
⁶ _____ every culture.

2 ◀) 2.11 **Read the words from the lecture and the definitions. Then listen to the lecture again and match the words with the correct definition.**

1 fundamental ___   a a series of things arranged by importance
2 hierarchy ___   b to provide something that someone needs
3 satisfy ___   c to make certain that something happens
4 ensure ___   d relating to the basic nature of something

5 tier ___   e safety from attack, harm, or damage
6 shelter ___   f an idea
7 security ___   g a place to live
8 concept ___   h one of several rows, layers, or levels

3 **Compare your answers with a partner. Can you remember what helped you work out the meaning?**

Developing critical thinking

1 **Discuss these questions in a group.**

1 Make a list of things you've done and decisions you've made today. Which of the needs in Maslow's pyramid did each one satisfy?

2 According to Maslow's hierarchy, the lower needs must be satisfied before the higher ones. Do you agree with this? Why or why not? Can you think of any people who have satisfied the higher needs, but not lower ones?

2 **Think about the ideas from *What makes some people hoarders?* and *The hierarchy of needs* and discuss these questions in a group.**

1 Think of some possessions that many people think are important. Which of Maslow's needs do these things satisfy?

2 Do you think there are any needs that possessions cannot satisfy? What are they? Why can't possessions satisfy them?

Vocabulary skill

> **USEFUL LANGUAGE**
> the need for respect/security/ safety
> the need to be the best you can be
> belong to a family/group/ community

FORMAL AND INFORMAL LANGUAGE

When learning new vocabulary, find out whether the word or expression is primarily used in formal situations, informal situations, or is appropriate for both. It is important not to use too much formal vocabulary in informal conversations, or to use informal language in very formal or academic situations.

Many formal or academic words have informal synonyms:

*Hoarding is when your **possessions** impair your ability to live your life.* (formal)

*There is **stuff** everywhere—newspapers, clothing, scraps of paper, old toys.* (informal)

***Establishing** a filing system is a good start.* (formal)

*She **set up** a filing system with Dr. Taylor and dramatically reduced the clutter.* (informal)

1 Look at these words from *What makes some people hoarders?* and *The hierarchy of needs*. What do they mean? Which are more formal? Which are more informal? Use a dictionary to help you.

| categorize | dramatically | help | identify | make sure | numerous |

2 Look at the sentences. The words in bold are either too formal or too informal for the context. Replace them with a word from exercise 1.

1 Studies indicate that the number of patients with hoarding disorders has increased **a lot** in the last decade.
2 Hey, Tom, can you **ensure** you turn off the lights when you go out?
3 According to the research, people with hoarding disorders struggle to **put** objects **in groups**.
4 I'm lost! Can you **assist** me?
5 Leila's paper **picks out** several potential problems with Maslow's theory.
6 Maslow's work organizes **a lot of** human motivations into a single theory.

3 Discuss the questions with a partner. Use informal vocabulary.

1 Describe a friend or family member who you admire. What does this person do, and why do you admire him or her? What do you think drives this person?
2 Make a list of some basic needs that still haven't been satisfied for many people in the world. What can be done to improve this situation?

4 Join another pair and share your answers to the questions in exercise 3. Imagine you are presenting your answer to a larger group in a formal context. Use formal vocabulary in your answers.

> **THINK ABOUT:**
> clean water
> electricity
> food
> housing

SPEAKING Presentation on personal and community values

You are going to learn how to use a variety of useful comparative forms, how to use the weak pronunciation of *as*, and how to make repairs and correct your own mistakes while speaking. You are then going to use these skills to describe the needs and values that are most important to you and your community.

Grammar

MAKING COMPARISONS

the ... the

In spoken and written English, people often use *the* + comparative + *the* + comparative to mean, 'If it is more X, it will be more Y.'

Establishing a filing system is a good start. **The sooner, the better**. (= It is best to start right away.)

The longer *I waited,* **the harder** *it was to change.* (= As time passed, it became harder to change.)

Comparative forms of compound adjectives

If the first word of the compound is an adjective (**open** minded, **long** lasting), use -er or *more* to make the comparative form. If the first word is not an adjective (**badly** behaved), use *more*.

First, at the bottom, are the **lower-level** *physiological needs.*

I'd like a **more expensive-looking** *car.*

A **more culturally-sensitive** *theory would include ideas like these.*

1 Complete the sentences with *a/an*, *as*, *more*, *the*, or *-er*. If nothing is needed in a blank, write **X**.

   1 A problem for hoarders is that _____ messier their homes are, _____ _____ depressed they feel.

   2 Money can make you happy for a short time, but _____ long _____ - lasting happiness comes from friends and family.

   3 To use your time most wisely, experts advise us to do our _____ high _____ -priority tasks earlier in the day, when we are more alert.

   4 According to Maslow's theory, _____ high _____ a need is on the pyramid, _____ _____ valuable it is.

   5 To overcome their problems, most hoarders need the support of their family and friends. _____ more, _____ better.

2 Complete the sentences with your own ideas and opinions. Use comparative forms with *the … the*. Work in pairs to compare ideas.

   1 In my opinion, the richer you are, …

   2 The older you are, …

   3 The bigger your family is, …

   4 The more stressful your job is, …

   5 The more beautiful/handsome you are, …

3 Complete the questions with the comparative form of the compound adjective in parentheses.

   1 Would you do a _____ (low-paying) job if it was really interesting?

   2 If you could improve one thing about yourself, would you rather be _____ (good-looking) or _____ (well-educated)?

   3 Are you _____ (open-minded) now than when you were a child?

   4 Which is a _____ (high-priority) need for you, your career or your family?

   5 Which experience do you think is _____ (life-changing): starting university, starting a new career, or starting a family?

4 Work with a partner. Ask and answer the questions in exercise 3.

Pronunciation skill

▎**WEAK FORM OF *AS*** ▰▰▰▰▰▰▰▰▰▰▰▰▰▰▰▰

In comparisons, the pronunciation of the word *as* is often 'weak' and sounds like /əz/. It can be difficult to hear this difference, but it is important to listen for it in order to better understand lectures and conversations.

*Water is a vital need, **as** we cannot live without it.* (strong = /æz/)

*For non-hoarders, throwing out newspapers isn't **as** difficult.* (weak = /əz/)

1 🔊 2.12 Listen and repeat the examples in the box above.

2 🔊 **2.13 Listen to the sentences from *What makes some people hoarders?* and *The hierarchy of needs*. Circle the weak forms of *as*.**

1 They have difficulties categorizing and making decisions, **as** Dr. Taylor noted earlier.
2 It wasn't **as** hard **as** I'd thought it would be.
3 I'll write some needs for each level of the pyramid, and you can suggest some, **as** well.
4 That's **as** basic **as** you can get.
5 If you're a painter, you want to be **as** good **as** you can.
6 There's also the need to help the group **as** a whole succeed.

3 **Work with a partner. Discuss the questions below. Make comparisons in your answers. Listen and check your partner's pronunciation of the weak form of *as*.**

1 Are your friends as important to you as your family? Why or why not?
2 Describe a good friend. How are you and your friend similar or different?
3 Do you think your studies are going as well as they could?

Speaking skill

MAKING REPAIRS

Everyone makes mistakes when speaking. If you realize you have made an error or someone else points out a problem with something you've said, you can use an expression such as *I mean ...*, *sorry*, *uh*, *oh*, or *um*. Then correct the error.

*This newspaper is an interesting article – **uh**, it <u>has</u> a very interesting article.*

1 🔊 **2.14 Listen and complete the conversation. Notice how the speakers make repairs. Then practice the conversation with a partner.**

A: Do you mind giving me a hand?
B: Yes, I ... I _____, no, I don't mind at all. What would you like me to do?
A: Could you help me move this armchair, _____, this couch?
B: Oh right! What a ... _____, I can see why you need help!

2 **Practice the conversation with a partner. The words in bold are wrong. Say the mistakes and repair them, using an expression from above.**

A: Have you **see** this story in the paper?
B: No. **What it** about?
A: It's about this survey. They asked kids what they want to be when they grow up. And the top answer **were** 'famous'.
B: Wow, that's **depressed**.
A: I know. When I was a kid I **want** to be a teacher or a doctor.
B: Well, I guess TV **have** really changed people's needs and values.

SPEAKING TASK

Compare your values and the values of your community.

Audience: classmates/peers
Context: an academic presentation
Purpose: to describe your personal values and compare them with the prevailing values of your community

BRAINSTORM

Work in groups. What needs and values affect people's decisions and lifestyles? Think about the ideas from *What makes some people hoarders?* and *The hierarchy of needs*. Add your ideas to the ones below.

FAME
RESPECT
FOOD
WEALTH
EDUCATION
BEAUTY
POWER
FINANCIAL SECURITY
COMMUNITY
CHILDREN
TAKING CARE OF ELDERS
LOVE
INDEPENDENCE
SHELTER
FRIENDS

PLAN

Think about the values you discussed. Which five values are most important to you personally? Which are most important to the majority of the people in your community? Rank them from 1 (most important) to 5 (least important).

My personal values	My community's values
1 _____	1 _____
2 _____	2 _____
3 _____	3 _____
4 _____	4 _____
5 _____	5 _____

SPEAK

Work in pairs. Give a presentation on the values you chose. Discuss the following points and more. Use comparisons and the weak form of *as*. If you make any mistakes, repair them.

- Which values are most important to you?
- Which are most important to your community?
- How are your values and your community's values different?
- What do you think is the reason for these differences?

SHARE

Compare your ideas in groups. Which values did most people choose? Can your group agree on a list of the top five values for the community?

USEFUL LANGUAGE

a high priority
an important concept
For me …
Instead, …
On the other hand, …
more/less important
Personally, …

STUDY SKILLS   Getting the most out of classes

Getting started

Discuss these questions with a partner.

1 What do you do to prepare before you listen in class?
2 What do you do during class? What are you thinking about while the professor or your classmates are speaking?
3 What do you do if you don't understand something in class?
4 How often do you speak in class?

Scenario

Read the scenario. Why do you think the professor thought Jun was unhappy? What are some things Jun can do to get more out of his classes?

Jun is a first-year Communications major. He knows that listening carefully in class is very important to his success in university and he deeply respects his professors. He always reads the textbook or handouts before class. During class, he listens quietly. If he doesn't understand something, he writes the question in his notes so that he can research it after class. He is very embarrassed by some of the other students in his courses, who frequently interrupt the professor to ask questions, make comments, or even disagree with the professor. While the other students are talking or giving their opinions, Jun uses this time to read and review the notes he has taken so far. Recently, one of Jun's professors said to him, 'You seem very unhappy with this course. What is the matter?' This comment was very confusing to him, since he liked the professor and the class very much.

Consider it

Look at these tips for participating in class. Which ones does Jun already do? Which do you think can help Jun get more out of his classes?

1 **Prepare** Do any assigned reading from handouts or the textbook before class. If you have questions about the reading, write them down before class.
2 **Stay focused** To keep your mind from wandering, focus on understanding the main ideas. Also listen for answers to the questions you wrote down before class.
3 **Listen actively** As the professor is speaking, ask yourself: Do I understand this idea? How is it similar to other ideas we have studied in class? Do I agree with the professor's point of view?
4 **Ask questions** Some professors prefer to answer questions as they go, while others take questions at the end of the lecture.
5 **Participate** If there is an opportunity for discussion, share your views. Also listen respectfully to your classmates' ideas and try to understand them.

Over to you

Discuss these questions with a partner.

1 Which of the things above do you already do?
2 Which of the tips do you think will be most useful to you?
3 What are some other things you can do to get more out of your classes?

LISTENING	Listening for organization
	Listening to interpret the speaker's attitude
VOCABULARY	Word + preposition combinations
SPEAKING	Fielding questions during a presentation
PRONUNCIATION	Using contrastive stress for emphasis

Discussion point

Discuss these questions with a partner.

1   Think about a typical day. How many different sounds do you hear from the moment you wake up until you go to sleep?

2   What are your favorite sounds?

3   Do you associate any sounds with favorite places or memories from your childhood?

Vocabulary preview

1 Read the sentences. Circle the word or phrase closest in meaning to the word in bold.

1 When we listen to speech, we are able to **anticipate** the next sounds we will hear.

   a believe   **b** expect

2 We were **distracted** by the loud noise outside the window, making it difficult to concentrate on our homework.

   a drawn away   **b** decreased

3 The noise seemed to **magnify** by the minute. Eventually, it got so loud we couldn't continue our conversation.

   a demand   **b** intensify

4 Dogs can **perceive** very high sounds that people can't hear.

   a detect   **b** complete

5 The sound **persisted** all night. We wondered if it would ever stop.

   a attempted   **b** continued

6 The noise from the stadium disturbed the families who lived in close **proximity** to it.

   a supplies   **b** nearness

7 I don't know what's wrong with my computer. It's making all these **random** sounds.

   a without pattern **b** slowly

8 The alarm was **unpredictable**. It kept stopping and starting, so we didn't know what to expect.

   a changeable   **b** responsible

LISTENING 1 That's so annoying!

Before you listen

1 Which of these sounds bother you? Check (✓) your answers. Compare with a partner.

☐ a plane flying overhead   ☐ a smoke alarm
☐ a baby crying   ☐ loud bird song
☐ a dentist's drill   ☐ someone eating
☐ a dog barking   ☐ someone else's mp3 player
☐ a fly buzzing   ☐ someone typing

2 When was the last time you were bothered by one of these sounds?

Global listening

> **LISTENING FOR ORGANIZATION**
>
> There are many ways a speaker may let you know how the information you are about to hear will be organized. For example:
>
> *We'll focus on four reasons for …*
>
> *Let's consider three factors …*
>
> *Two examples of this are …*
>
> These number signal phrases tell you what to listen for. Use them to help you follow the ideas you hear and to organize your notes.

🔊 2.15 **Read the factors that can make a sound annoying. Then listen and number the factors in the order the speaker presents them.**

ACADEMIC KEYWORDS

attempt	(v)	/ə'tempt/
consider	(v)	/kən'sɪdər/
factor	(n)	/'fæktər/

___ regular, repetitive

___ unpredictability

___ uncertainty about how long it will last

___ the pitch

Close listening

1 🔊 2.15 **Listen again.** Circle **the ideas that the speaker mentions to explain the factors.**

  1 Strangers' phone calls are annoying because **they are often loud / we don't know when they will end**.

  2 A dripping faucet is annoying because it is **repetitive / continuous** and persists.

  3 A sound seems to magnify because it **is loud / doesn't stop**.

  4 The sound of the fly will vary because it moves in **an unpredictable way / in circular patterns**.

  5 The sound of fingernails scraping on a blackboard are annoying mostly because of the **high / low** sounds.

2 **Work with a partner. Answer the questions.**

  1 According to the speaker, a dripping faucet and fingernails scraping on a chalkboard seem *universally annoying*. What do you think this means?

  2 According to the speaker, which factor do a dripping faucet and fingernails scraping have in common?

Developing critical thinking

Discuss these questions in a group.

1 Which reasons do you find the most compelling for explaining why some sounds are annoying? What other reasons can make a sound annoying? Think of some examples.

2 In cities we are surrounded by many sounds. We know that noise can cause stress. What can we do to reduce the annoying sounds that we make?

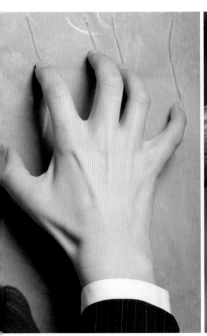

LISTENING 2 Was that my phone ringing?

Before you listen

Answer the questions. Then compare with a partner, trying to give possible explanations.

1 When someone says they feel hungry or warm, do you start to feel that way also?
2 Have you ever awakened in the night and felt like you couldn't move?
3 Have you ever heard a sound in a dream and thought it was real?
4 Have you ever been in a crowd, and felt sure you heard someone call your name, but no one actually did?

Global listening

🔊 2.16 **Listen to the podcast *Was that my phone ringing?* Then answer the questions with a partner.**

1 What is a phantom phone ring?
2 According to the podcast, what is phantom vibration syndrome?
3 What are phantom words?
4 How many studies were cited to explain the phenomenon of phantom words?

Close listening

1 🔊 2.16 **Listen to the podcast again and complete the notes.**

Phantom rings
Reason 1 - brain trying to process [1]_____
Reason 2 - [2]_____ *caused by anticipating the sound*

Phantom vibrations
Main reason - phone carried [3]_____, *always set to vibrate so brain anticipates vibration*

Phantom words
Main reason -brain trying to makes sense of [4]_____
  Study 1 - volunteers listened to a recording of repeated [5]_____ *and then asked to recall words. Many reported hearing words that* [6]_____
  Study 2 - [7]_____ *of different nationalities listened to English recording. Many reported hearing words from their* [8]_____

LISTENING TO INTERPRET THE SPEAKER'S ATTITUDE

As you listen, pay attention to the descriptive words the speaker uses to present ideas and details. This will help you understand not only the facts presented, but the speaker's attitude toward the information. For example, phrases such as: *a stranger variation, interestingly, ..., that isn't likely, ... It seems, ... Perhaps ...*

After you finish listening, review the details you understood. Ask yourself how the various ideas are connected, and what the speaker's attitude is toward them.

ACADEMIC KEYWORDS

experience	(v)	/ɪkˈspɪriəns/
interpret	(v)	/ɪnˈtɜrprət/
variation	(n)	/ˌveriˈeɪʃ(ə)n/

2 🔊 2.16 **Listen again. Decide if the sentences are *T* (true) or *F* (false) according to the speaker. Work with partner to correct any statements to make them true.**

1 Phantom rings are a curious example of how our brain processes sounds. ___
2 Researchers seem to understand why phantom phone rings are common. ___
3 People have reported hearing phantom rings while dreaming. ___
4 The speaker thinks people's desire to get a call, may cause the phantom ring. ___
5 The speaker thinks phantom phone syndrome would be irritating. ___
6 People all heard the same common words on the recordings. ___
7 In the study, language learners listened to the recording one time. ___
8 The speaker seemed to think the results of the study were interesting. ___
9 Judging from the conclusion, the speaker thinks we should decrease phone use. ___

Developing critical thinking

1 **Discuss these questions in a group.**

1 Why do you think the language learners experienced what they did in the study? Have you experienced this while listening to English? Describe what you heard.
2 Have you had any experience or do you know any other stories of the mind playing tricks on us in this way (e.g. remembering things wrongly, or imagining we see things)? What do you think the reasons for these are?

2 **Think about the ideas from *That's so annoying* and *Was that my phone ringing?* and discuss these questions in a group.**

1 Research suggests that if you are put in a chamber with no sound at all, some people hate it. Why would that be? Do you think you would like it? Is it possible to have no sound at all?
2 Think about what assaults our senses in the modern world as compared to 100 years ago. How would it have been different? Complete the table with ✓ or ✗ and then justify your reasons to the group.

	Now	100 years ago
noisier/quieter		
smellier / less smelly		
uglier / more beautiful environment		
tastier / less tasty food		

Vocabulary skill

WORD + PREPOSITION COMBINATIONS

Some words are often followed by a particular preposition (sometimes called a dependent preposition). It is useful to learn these words together. These combinations can be:

Adjective + preposition

*You may be **unaware of** the conversation.*

Verb + preposition

*You can **relate to** what I'm saying.*

Noun + preposition

*Our brain tries to make **sense out of** meaningless noise.*

1 🔊 2.17 **Complete the text with the prepositions in the box. Then listen and check.**

by	from	of	to

The frequency (1)_____ a sound is different from the loudness of a sound. The frequency is the rate at which a sound wave vibrates. Examples (2)_____ low frequency sounds are a deep male voice, and the rumble of thunder during a storm. In contrast, examples of high frequency sounds are a squeaky door, and a woman's high voice. There is a limited range (3)_____ sounds humans can hear. Scientists have found that humans are more sensitive (4)_____ low frequency sounds, and that high frequency sounds are harder to hear as people get older. Hearing loss is a part (5)_____ the aging process: however, chronic exposure (6)_____ loud sounds also contributes (7)_____ hearing loss. Researchers have found that people who listen (8)_____ an mp3 player continuously often suffer (9)_____ hearing loss. They've also found that this can be prevented (10)_____ turning off the music for about five minutes every hour. This brief rest allows the ears to recover (11)_____ the sound.

2 **Discuss these questions with a partner.**

1 Do you listen to an mp3 player? If so, how many hours per day, on average?

2 What are loud sounds that might contribute to hearing loss?

SPEAKING Presentation of a plan for a public place

You are going to learn two ways to emphasize information in a sentence: cleft sentences and contrastive stress. You will also learn the speaking skill of fielding questions after a presentation. You are going to use these to conduct a survey, then present your findings to your classmates.

Grammar

CLEFT SENTENCES

You can use a cleft sentence in conversation to highlight information you want someone to focus on. Structurally, you move to the beginning of the sentence what is most important.

Form	Example
It + verb *to be* + important information + the remainder of the sentence	**It's stress that** makes you hear the phantom ring. **It was Shin who** kept hearing the sound. (No one else.) **It's Tuesday** we have an exam, not Wednesday.

1 **Work with a partner. Practice the conversations and identify the cleft sentences.**

  1 **A:** Did Amin say he would meet us at the library?
    B: No, it was at the science center.
  2 **A:** Hey, I got a text from Nina that she's coming to visit this Tuesday.
    B: I got a text, too. Her plans changed. It's Wednesday she's coming.
  3 **A:** I'm worried about the grammar section of the exam.
    B: It's the reading section that's difficult for me.
  4 **A:** Loud sounds don't annoy me. I grew up in a big city surrounded by noise.
    B: Yeah. It's soft sounds that get to me—like the quiet ticking of a clock.

2 **Complete the first conversation. Practice with a partner. Then role play conversations 2, 3 and 4 using cleft constructions.**

  1 **A:** Did you hear about Ana? She heard shouting in the apartment next door last night.
    B: I talked to her this morning. It was _____ she heard. [say another sound] She said it was quite scary.
  2 **A:** It looks like Khalil left his phone here.
    B: I checked with him. It isn't Khalil's. … [Say it was someone else who left it. Say how you know.]
  3 **A:** I didn't see Lee in class on Monday. Maybe because of the storm.
    B: … [Agree and specify what exactly the problem was connected to the storm and what the consequences were.]
  4 **A:** I couldn't concentrate with that fly buzzing around the room.
    B: … [Say that it was another sound that was more annoying. Add comment to say why.]

Pronunciation skill

USING CONTRASTIVE STRESS FOR EMPHASIS

English has regular stress patterns. The most important content words are stressed in a sentence. You can emphasize an idea by shifting the stress from the regular stress pattern. You can do this in different ways depending on what you want to focus on:

Regular stress: **DAN** drinks coffee while he's studying.

To emphasize what: Dan drinks **COFFEE** while he's studying.

To emphasize when: Dan drinks coffee while he's **STUDYING**.

1 🔊 2.18 **Listen to the sentences. Underline the contrasted words. Practice with a partner.**

1 Low sounds actually affect us more than high sounds.
2 Our ears don't identify the sounds we hear, our brains do.
3 Jung complained about the noise, but it didn't bother Wei.
4 Adan was annoyed by his neighbor's radio, not by his TV.
5 Aida heard so many phantom rings that she ignored a real call.

2 🔊 2.19 **Listen again. Match each sentence 1–4 with the correct meaning a–d.**

1 ___   a Lara's is worse, though.
2 ___   b His old ring tone wasn't quite as bad.
3 ___   c It didn't affect the rest of her family.
4 ___   d At night it wasn't as loud.

Speaking skill

FIELDING QUESTIONS DURING A PRESENTATION

To give the listener an opportunity to ask questions

Are there any questions?   Is anything unclear?   Did you understand everything about …?

Repeating the question

You asked what I meant by …   The question was [repeat the question].

Follow-up information

That's a good question. Let me explain / be clearer /give you an example.

1 🔊 2.20 **Listen and complete these sentences using phrases from the skill box.**

1 **A:** OK, _____?
    B: Student 1: Yes, what is 'pitch'?
    A: _____: What is pitch? Pitch means how high or low a sound is.

2 **A:** What sound did you say is the most annoying?
    B: _____ what sound I said is the most annoying, correct?

3 **A:** Do some sounds become less annoying if we hear them every day?
    B: That's _____. I'm not sure.

4 **A:** That's all the information we gathered. _____ what I said about our group's conclusion?
    B: Not exactly.

2 **Work with a partner. Take turns to review one of the listenings. Practice asking and fielding questions.**

SPEAKING TASK

Work in a group to consider ways to make access to quiet, natural places available to people in cities.

Audience:	classmates
Context:	an academic presentation
Purpose:	to synthesize ideas learned in the unit, apply them to a practical, real world scenario, and present design ideas in a presentation format

BRAINSTORM

Imagine your group is going to plan a park where people can relax and enjoy pleasant sounds. Compile lists of noise pollution problems in cities, and pleasant sounds you think are important for people to be able to hear. List at least four ideas in each category.

Problems	Pleasant sounds

PLAN

Plan a presentation on a park design you think would take into consideration different age groups and the types of activities they enjoy. Follow these steps:

1 Organize a summary of the urban noise problems you've identified.
2 Make notes on how the park would be designed to eliminate noises issues and provide a relaxing space. For each feature, include enough details to make your plan clear to your audience.
3 Make a simple drawing to explain the design of the park.

Features in the park	Details of each feature

SPEAK

Present your plan to other groups. Pause to field questions and to explain any ideas someone tells you are unclear. Remember to use cleft sentences and contrastive word stress for emphasis.

SHARE

Return to your group. Compare the ideas that other groups had. Then share your conclusions about what would be a successful urban space.

Revision strategies

by Stella Cottrell

A good approach to revision requires creativity, interactive study techniques, a high degree of motivation, time management, working well with others, writing skills, and being able to use your powers of selectivity, critical thinking, and memory. Keep revision in mind for the whole term or year.

Tick the boxes beside specific revision activities listed below if you consider that they would help you.

☐ Make your notes clear, visual, colorful, dynamic, and memorable. Leave lots of space to add new information later in the term.

☐ Make up index cards of key information as you go along.

☐ Go over your work at regular intervals so that you have less to do at the last minute.

Use time carefully

☐ Start as early in the year as possible.
☐ Draw up a revision timetable.
☐ Organise your priorities—make a list and rate them according to how important they are.
☐ Make a Time Circle for revision by drawing a circle, dividing it into 24 segments to represent 24 hours, and shading it to show how you plan to divide your time.
☐ Use spare moments for revision.

Keep a positive attitude

☐ Work on your motivation and your attitude towards exams.
☐ Regard difficulties as challenges for which you can devise new strategies.

Work with others

☐ Arrange revision sessions with friends.

Ask for help

☐ Find out from tutors how exam answers differ from course essays.

Use memory triggers

☐ Research techniques for improving memorization using memory triggers.
☐ Cut down your notes to key points, key words, and memory triggers.
☐ Learn by heart essential information only, such as dates, names, and formulae.

Revise by ear

☐ Record yourself answering questions— listening to your own voice can help memory.

Stay healthy

☐ Sleep, relax, and take plenty of breaks.

Use exam papers from previous years

☐ Check which questions come up regularly.
☐ Brainstorm answers to past questions.
☐ Make outline plans for as many questions as you can.
☐ Time yourself writing some of these, to build writing speed and for general practice.
☐ Discuss questions with others. Work out plans together.
☐ Consider in advance what detail needs to be left out of exam answers.

Tomorrow

THE SYNDIC BY C.M. KORNBLUTH : MOB RULE IN USA

160 PAGES!

DECEMBER 1953 35c

LISTENING	Listening for problems and solutions
	Recognizing definitions
VOCABULARY	Prefixes and suffixes with special meanings
SPEAKING	Describing a word you do not know
PRONUNCIATION	Expressing surprise vs. asking for confirmation

Discussion point

Discuss these questions with a partner.

1 The image above shows how people in the 1950s thought life in the future would be. What did they get right? What did they get wrong? Do you think predictions about the future are usually reliable? Why or why not?

2 Imagine yourself five years from now. What will your life be like? What will be different from now?

3 What are three future events that you're looking forward to? Is there anything you're *not* looking forward to?

Vocabulary preview

1 Complete the sentences with the words in the box.

address   century   demographic   overpopulation   pension   planet

1 Global warming is a critical issue we need to _____ now.

2 There is a good chance that Mars, the _____ most similar to Earth, has life on it.

3 I think people will travel everywhere in flying cars in the 22nd _____.

4 In my country, most people receive a _____ from the government after they retire.

5 According to _____ studies, the population in my country is becoming more diverse.

6 I'm not worried about _____ in the future. The number of people on Earth won't increase that much.

2 Work with a partner. Do you agree with the sentences in exercise 1? Change the sentences if necessary to make them true for you.

LISTENING 1 A rapidly aging population

Before you listen

What is life like for older people in your country now? Check (✓) the sentences that are true where you live.

- [ ] **1** The number of older people is growing rapidly.
- [ ] **2** Older people usually live with their children and grandchildren.
- [ ] **3** Respect for older people is an important part of the culture.
- [ ] **4** Older people receive a pension from the government.
- [ ] **5** People usually retire at age 55.
- [ ] **6** Older people spend a lot of time traveling and enjoying outdoor activities.
- [ ] **7** A lot of people live to be over 100.

Global listening

LISTENING FOR PROBLEMS AND SOLUTIONS

Lectures, news reports, and other sources of information often include a discussion of problems that may result from a situation, and possible ways to solve these problems. The problem is usually mentioned first, followed by one or more solutions. When listening, it's a good idea to write the problem and its solutions together in your notes.

1 🔊 **2.21** **You are going to hear a conversation about the worldwide increase in the number of older people. Look at the speakers' notes for their presentation. Circle the problems and solutions they mention.**

Problems

1 *It will be harder for young people to find jobs.*
2 *Pension programs will have problems.*
3 *More older people will live alone.*
4 *The environment will be harmed.*

Solutions

a *Governments can build housing for older people.*
b *Governments can raise taxes.*
c *Hospitals can hire nurses from abroad.*
d *Older people can work longer.*
e *Older people can live with their children and grandchildren.*
f *Governments can develop clean energy.*

2 Look at the answers you circled in exercise 1. Match the problems with their solutions. Compare answers with a partner.

Close listening

🔊 **2.21 Listen again and make inferences based on the information in the conversation. Which of these statements are probably true?**

☐ **1** Both speakers have read the UN report on aging.
☐ **2** In the future, a majority of elderly people will be centenarians.
☐ **3** Health care for older people will be less expensive in the future.
☐ **4** Women often live longer than their husbands.
☐ **5** In the speakers' country, people do not often live with their grandparents.

Developing critical thinking

Discuss these questions in a group.

1 Give a summary of the conversation. Do the speakers think the aging population is generally a good thing or a bad thing? What benefits, problems, and solutions do they discuss?
2 What can you infer about the attitudes toward older people in the speakers' culture? How does this compare with those of your culture?

ACADEMIC KEYWORDS		
contribute	(v)	/kənˈtrɪbjut/
report	(n)	/rɪˈpɔrt/
trend	(n)	/trend/

USEFUL LANGUAGE

crime

education

family structure

health care

the economy

the labor market

values

LISTENING 2 Our next planet?

Before you listen

Discuss these questions in a group.

1 Think about life on planet Earth. What conditions make it possible for people to live on this planet? Make a list.

2 Do you think it will still be possible for people to live on Earth in 100 years? What about in 1,000 years? Why or why not?

THINK ABOUT:

temperature

atmosphere

natural resources

other plants and animals

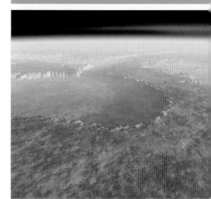

Global listening

1 🔊 2.22 **Listen to a radio news program about humans living on Mars in the future. What problems do the people mention? Check (✓) the sentences.**

☐ 1 The Earth will be too crowded in the future.

☐ 2 The environment on Earth will have serious problems.

☐ 3 The supply of oil on Earth will run out by the year 2100.

☐ 4 Mars is currently too cold for human life.

☐ 5 There isn't enough air to breathe on Mars.

☐ 6 Mars is approximately half the size of Earth.

☐ 7 It could be thousands of years before humans can live on Mars.

☐ 8 Not everyone would be able to move to Mars.

2 **Look at the problems you checked in exercise 1. Do the speakers suggest solutions to all of these problems? Which problems didn't have solutions?**

Close listening

RECOGNIZING DEFINITIONS

In formal contexts, experts often use words that they know will not be familiar to many of their listeners. In these cases, they often give a brief definition of the term. In news reports, it is very common for the interviewer to interrupt politely to ask for or offer a definition of an unfamiliar term. To recognize these definitions, listen for key words such as: *or, that is, in other words, which is, refer to, by X, you mean …,* and more.

*Dr. Elaine Hines is an **astrobiologist—that is**, someone who studies life on other planets.*

Some definitions also appear directly after the unfamiliar word, without any key words to introduce them.

*But right now Mars isn't **habitable. It can't support life.***

🔊 2.23 **Listen to the excerpts from the news report. Match the words with the correct definition.**

1 atmosphere ____
2 terraforming ____
3 greenhouse gases ____
4 carbon dioxide ____
5 oxygen ____
6 astronaut ____

a someone who travels in space
b making a place more similar to Earth
c the air around a planet
d a gas humans need to breathe
e gases responsible for global warming
f CO_2, a gas causing higher temperatures on Earth

ACADEMIC KEYWORDS

amount	(n)	/əˈmaʊnt/
process	(n)	/ˈprɑses/
relatively	(adv)	/ˈrelətɪvli/

Developing critical thinking

1 Discuss these questions in a group.

1 Which do you think would be easier: to solve the problems we currently face on Earth, or to make another planet habitable? Why?

2 Would you want to live on another planet? Why or why not? Make a list of advantages and disadvantages. Which advantage or disadvantage is the most important?

2 Think about the ideas from *A rapidly aging population* and *Our next planet?* and discuss these questions in a group.

1 Do you think an aging population will have a positive or negative effect on issues like population growth and global warming? Why? Can you think of other problems and benefits that haven't been mentioned?

2 Think about how technology has changed in the last hundred years. How can technology improve life in the future? How could it make life in the future worse?

USEFUL LANGUAGE

contribute to science

deal with isolation

experience new things

make history

miss friends and family

THINK ABOUT:

education

health care

space exploration

war and conflict

Vocabulary skill

PREFIXES AND SUFFIXES WITH SPECIAL MEANINGS

Many English words have prefixes or suffixes that come from Greek or Latin. This is especially common in academic and scientific language. Each of these prefixes or suffixes has a special meaning that can help you guess the meaning of an unfamiliar word. In this example from *A rapidly aging population*, the prefix *cent-* come from the Latin word for *hundred*.

A: What do you call people who are over 100?

B: Oh, you mean **cent**enarians.

A: That's it, *centenarians*. ... *Centenarians*, like the *cent-* in *century*.

There are dozens of these prefixes and suffixes in English. Here are some common ones.

Prefix or suffix	Meaning	Examples
con/co-	with, together	*connect, cooperate*
-form	shape	*reform, deform*
-graph	write	*autograph, photograph*
-logy	study of	*biology, geology*
-port	carry	*export, import*
-sphere	ball	*atmosphere, hemisphere*
tele-	distance	*television, telescope*

1 Look at the words below. Match the prefixes and suffixes in bold with their meanings.

1 **bio**logy, **bio**graphy ____
2 **eco**logy, **eco**nomics ____
3 **geo**logy, **geo**graphy ____
4 **multi**cultural, **multi**ply ____
5 **phys**ics, **phys**ician ____

a earth
b life
c the body
d environment
e many

2 🔊 **2.24 Listen to the sentences from** *A rapidly aging population* **and** *Our next planet?* **Complete the sentences with the correct prefixes and suffixes.**

1 … a lot to _____ tribute …

2 … mental or _____ ical.

3 _____ logists say …

4 … is an astro _____ logist …

5 … size and _____ logy.

6 … have an atmo _____ , …

7 … trans _____ ing people …

8 … can't just _____ port people …

3 **Use the prefixes and suffixes in the skills box and exercise 1 to complete the questions below. Then discuss the questions with a partner.**

1 Which form of communication do you think will have a bigger effect on our lives in the future: _____ vision, mobile _____ phones, or the Internet?

2 Are many houses in your town or city built with _____ friendly products that don't harm the environment?

3 Do you live in the southern or the northern hemi _____ ? How do you think life is different in the other hemi _____ ?

4 Do you own any _____ able devices like an ebook reader or an mp3 player? How have these devices changed the way we live?

5 How often do you read _____ graphies? Make a list of people whose lives would be interesting to read about.

SPEAKING Presentation about future problems

You are going to learn how to use the future perfect to talk about events that will happen by a certain time in the future, how to describe a word that you don't know or can't recall, and how to use intonation patterns to express surprise or ask for confirmation. You are then going to use these skills to talk about the most important problems people will face in the future.

Grammar

THE FUTURE PERFECT

Use the future perfect to talk about events and accomplishments that will happen by or before a point in the future. The future perfect is often used with time expressions with *by* and *before*. Use the future perfect when the exact time of the future event is not known or not important. If there is a specific time, use the future simple or future continuous.

Form	Example
will + *have* + past participle	The world's population **will have reached** 10 billion by the year 2050.
	I hope the pension programs **won't have run out** of money before I retire.
	The polar ice caps **will have melted** by then. (future perfect; we don't know the specific time when they will melt)
	The conference **will take place** in January of next year. (future simple; there is a specific time when the event happens)

1 Complete the sentences with the future simple or future perfect form of the verb in parentheses.

1 By 2050, people _____ to Mars and back at least once. (travel)

2 More people _____ in cities in the future. (live)

3 I'm afraid I _____ enough money by the time I retire. (not save)

4 The government _____ a new report on global warming next week. (release)

5 On Tuesday I _____ with this company for exactly two years. (be)

6 A group of scientists projects that sea levels _____ 60 centimeters by the year 2100. (rise)

7 Sara has come down with the flu, so she probably _____ at the party tomorrow. (not be)

8 I'm confident we _____ the big problems facing our planet by the time I'm old. (solve)

2 Discuss these questions with a partner. Use the future perfect.

1 What will you have accomplished by the end of this year?

2 What books are you reading these days? When will you have finished them?

3 Imagine yourself at age 75. What will you have accomplished by then? What will you *not* have done?

Speaking skill

DESCRIBING A WORD YOU DO NOT KNOW

In classroom discussions and other situations, it is common for all English speakers to forget a word (or simply not know it). In these cases, you can describe the meaning you want to express and ask for help with the word. People often begin with expressions such as *what do you call ...*, *how do you say ...*, *what's the word for ...*, or *what is it called when ...* .

A: And what about—uh, **what do you call** people who are over 100?

B: Oh, **you mean** 'centenarians'.

1 🔊 2.25 Complete the dialogues. Then listen and check. Practice the dialogues with a partner.

1 A: What do you _____ someone who looks for life on other planets?

   B: Oh, you _____ an astrobiologist.

2 A: Mars currently isn't ... sorry, what's _____ called _____ a place can't support life?

   B: Uninhabitable.

3 A: Excuse me, Professor Miller. What's the _____ for the air surrounding a planet?

   B: Do you _____ the atmosphere?

2 Look at the descriptions below. Can you remember the words? They all come from *A rapidly aging population* and *Our next planet?* Take turns describing the words with a partner.

1 a period of a hundred years: _____

2 a change or development over time: _____

3 a program that gives money to retired workers: _____

4 frozen water at the north and south poles: _____

5 changing a place so it is more like Earth: _____

6 the gases that cause global warming: _____

Pronunciation skill

INTONATION PATTERNS

Use a more extreme rising and falling intonation to show surprise. Use a more gently rising intonation to confirm what you heard.

A: *Jack's mother is 103 years old.*

B: *A hundred and three?* (= I can't believe it! That's surprising!)

B: *A hundred and three?* (= I didn't hear clearly.)

1 ◗ 2.26 Listen and repeat the excerpts from *A rapidly aging population* and *Our next planet?* Is the speaker expressing surprise or asking for confirmation? Write **S** (surprise) or **C** (confirmation).

1 **A:** Did you know that by 2050 there will be two billion people over 60 years old?

 B: Two billion? ___

2 **A:** There is an answer to this, however, which is a very long, very expensive process called *terraforming.*

 B: Terraforming? ___

3 **A:** To do this, you increase the amount of greenhouse gases on Mars.

 B: Greenhouse gases? ___

2 Complete the sentences with your own ideas. Work with a partner, reacting according to the meaning in parentheses.

1 I'm going to _____ before class tomorrow. (surprise)

2 I will get up at _____ o'clock tomorrow. (confirmation)

3 I'm going to visit _____ for vacation this year. (surprise)

4 I want to work as a _____ in the future. (confirmation)

5 I'm going to be _____ years old this year. (your own choice)

6 I'll graduate _____ months/years from now. (your own choice)

SPEAKING TASK

Work in a group to consider the most important problems people will face in the future.

Audience: classmates/peers
Context: an academic presentation
Purpose: to analyze future trends and describe future problems and solutions

BRAINSTORM

Think about what the world will be like 5 years, 20 years, and 50 years from now. What problems will people face? What progress will people have made? Discuss in groups and complete the chart.

	5 years	20 years	50 years
Problems			
Progress			

PLAN

Choose three future problems to talk about in a presentation. With a partner, think of possible solutions and write down key vocabulary related to each problem. Remember the phrases for asking about a word that you don't know or can't recall.

	Problem	Solutions	Key words
	Fifty years from now, we'll have run out of space for garbage.	• *use less plastic* • *recycle more*	*landfill* *packaging*
1			
2			
3			

THINK ABOUT:

crime and public safety
globalization
health care
military conflicts
natural resources
overpopulation
space exploration
technological advances
the economy

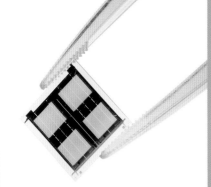

SPEAK

Work in groups. List your three problems and discuss ways to solve them.

SHARE

Return to your original partner and tell them some of the answers you heard. What were some interesting problems and solutions? Listen to your partner and use intonation to show surprise or ask for confirmation.

STUDY SKILLS Practicing speaking outside of class

Getting started

Discuss these questions with a partner.

1 How often do you speak English outside of class? When and where?

2 When you speak English outside of class, what are your aims?

3 Have you ever had a frustrating experience when you tried to use English outside of class? What happened?

Scenario

Read the scenario and try to think of three things Faisal could do to practice speaking outside of class more effectively.

Consider it

Look at these tips for practicing speaking outside of class. Which ones does Faisal already do? Which one do you think would help him the most?

1 **Find a language exchange partner or group** If you are in a small town, you can still go to a language-learning website to find people. You can also try local universities, community centers, coffee shops, and other places.

2 **You don't need to find a native speaker to practice** English is a language for international communication. Anyone who speaks the language (or is learning it) can give you an opportunity to practice.

3 **Prepare for your language exchange** Make a list of topics to discuss. You can also choose an article to read in advance and discuss together.

4 **Write down new words and expressions** If you hear a word that is useful or interesting to you, write it down and review it after you are finished talking.

5 **If you can't find a partner, practice listening** Many English-language radio broadcasts, movies, and TV programs are available online. Choose something interesting and enjoy it. Don't try to memorize it word for word.

6 **Have fun!** It's OK if you make mistakes or you don't catch every word you hear. Also, don't expect your conversation partner to be a skilled language teacher. Instead, focus on making friends and having a pleasant conversation.

Over to you

Discuss these questions with a partner.

1 Which of the things above do you already do?

2 Which of the tips do you think will be most useful to you?

3 What are some other ways to practice speaking outside of class?

Faisal is a second-year student majoring in international business. English is vital for his future career and he is determined to improve his speaking skills. He lives in a smaller city where there are not many native speakers of English, so he has few opportunities to practice. Some of his friends, co-workers, and classmates are also eager to practice English, but Faisal rarely speaks with them because he doesn't want to pick up a bad accent or learn incorrect English. Last semester, Faisal tried to have a language exchange with an Australian student, but it was an awkward and frustrating experience. They did not know what to talk about, and when they did speak, Faisal didn't understand everything he heard and made a few embarrassing mistakes. He asked the Australian very detailed questions about grammar, but he could not get any clear answers. Now, he mostly practices by listening to English news reports on TV and trying to copy down all of the words he hears. Then, to practice speaking, he repeats and memorizes the news report.

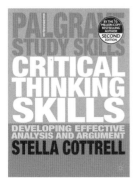
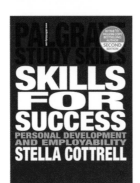

The phrases below give common ways of expressing useful functions. Use them to help you as you're completing the *Discussion points* and *Developing critical thinking* activities.

Asking for clarification

Sorry, can you explain that some more?
Could you say that another way?
When you say …, do you mean …?
Sorry, I don't follow that.
What do you mean?

Asking for repetition

Could you repeat that, please?
I'm sorry, I didn't catch that.
Could you say that again?

When you don't know the meaning of a word

What does … mean?
Sorry, I'm not sure what … means.

Working with a partner

Would you like to start?
Shall I go first?
Shall we do this one first?
Where do you want to begin?

Giving opinions

I think that …
It seems to me that …
In my opinion …
As I see it …

Agreeing and disagreeing

I know what you mean.
That's true.
You have a point there.
Yes. I see what you're saying, but …
I understand your point, but …
I don't think that's true.

Asking for opinions

Do you think …?
Do you feel …?
What do you think about …?
How about you, Jennifer? What do you think?
What about you?
Does anyone have any other ideas?
Do you have any thoughts on this?

Asking for more information

In what way?
Why do you think that?
Can you give an example?

Not giving a strong preference

It doesn't matter to me.
I don't really have a strong preference.
I've never really thought about that.
Either is fine.

Expressing interest

I'd like to hear more about that.
That sounds interesting.
How interesting!
Tell me more about that.

Giving reasons

This is … because …
This has to be … because …
I think … because …

Checking understanding

Do you know what I mean?
Do you see what I'm saying?
Are you following me?

Putting things in order

This needs to come first because …
I think this is the most/least important because …
For me, this is the most/least relevant because …

Preventing interruptions

Excuse me, I wasn't finished.
If I could just finish what I was saying…
Let me just finish this, please.
I haven't finished my thought/sentence.

Buying time

Let me think about that for a moment.
Let me gather my thoughts.
Just a minute. I need to think about that.

Clarifying

That's not exactly what I meant.
Sorry, I wasn't clear. Let me put it another way.
That isn't what I was trying to say.

The publishers would like to thank the following for their thoughtful insights and perceptive comments during the development of the material:

Belgium

Sylviane Granger, at CECL, University of Louvain
Magali Paquot

Egypt

Dr Gaber Khalil, AUC, Cairo

Germany

John Nixon at Universität Stuttgart

Japan

Robert Morton at Chuo University
Lesley Burda Ito

Oman

Mutaz Abumuaath at Nizwa College of Technology, Nizwa

Qatar

Jane Hoelker at Qatar University, Foundation English

Russia

Tatyana Gromoglasova, at the Siberian Institute of Management, Novosibirsk

Saudi Arabia

Dr Mohammed Al-Ahaydib and Dr Mohammed Hamdan at Imam Muhammad Ibn Saud University
Dr William Frawley, Education Experts
Heidi Omara

South Korea

Yoonji Kim, and Da Young Song at the Konkuk University Language Institute
Jina Kwon at Seoul National University

Taiwan

Laura Wang at Chung Yuan Christian University
Regina Jan at Lunghwa University of Science and Technology
Kitty Chu, Jessie Huang, Jenny Jen, and Wenyau Keng at the National Central University, Language Center
Sandrine Ting at the Department of Applied Foreign Language, St. John's University

Thailand

Wanpen Chaikitmongkol, Jindarat De Vleeschauwer, and Sonhsi Wichaidit at the English Division, Department of Western Languages and Humanities, Chiang Mai University

Turkey

Merve Oflaz at Bahcesehir University
Şahika Özkan-Tuğba Kın-Yadigar Aslan, Didem Gümüşlüoğlu, Meltem Sarandal, and Sibel Weeks at Doğuş University, İstanbul
Sevil Altikulaçoğlu, Sühendan Semine Er, Şerife Ersöz, Fatma Ünveren Gürocak at Gazi University
Deniz Ateşok at Istanbul Bilgi University
Ebru Yamaç at Maltepe University,
Aybike Oğuz at Özyeğin University

United Arab Emirates

Paul Barney, Doug Henderson, and Danielle Norris at Higher Colleges of Technology, Al Ain

United Kingdom

Nick Hillman at Anglia Ruskin University
Heather Abel and Richard Hillman at Bell London
Edward Bressan, Sara Hannam, and Stacey Hughes at Oxford Brookes University
Fiodhna Gardiner-Hyland at University of Limerick
Sally Morris, Ian Pople, and Simon Raw at University of Manchester
Averil Bolser and Peter Leverai at University of Nottingham, Ningbo
Jonathan Hadley

United States

Gail Schafers at Fontbonne Univeristy
Carole Mawson at Stanford University
Denise Mussman at University of Missouri
Abby Brown

Macmillan Education
Between Towns Road, Oxford OX4 3PP
A division of Macmillan Publishers Limited
Companies and representatives throughout the world

ISBN 978-0-230-42996-3

Text, design and illustration © Macmillan Publishers Limited 2013
Written by Mike Boyle and Ellen Kisslinger
Series Consultant Dorothy E. Zemach

The authors have asserted their rights to be identified as the authors
of this work in accordance with the Copyright, Design and Patents Act
1988.

First published 2013

Designed by emc design ltd
Illustrated by emc design ltd
Cover design by emc design ltd
Cover illustration/photograph by Thinkstock/iStockphoto
Picture research by Emily Taylor

The Academic Keyword List (AKL) was designed by Magali Paquot at
the Centre for English Corpus Linguistics, Université catholique de
Louvain (Belgium) within the framework of a research project led by
Professor Sylviane Granger.

http://www.uclouvain.be/en-372126.html

Authors' acknowledgements:

Mike Boyle
I am very grateful to the entire Macmillan Education team for their
guidance and insightful comments, and for the many ways in which
they have improved my work. I would also like to thank my wife for all
of her support and encouragement.

Ellen Kisslinger
I would like to thank the other authors of this course for their advice,
suggestions, and strong team effort made in the development of this
course. I would also like to thank the entire Macmillan Education
team for their guidance and support.

Special thanks to my daughter, Rachel Belanger, for her research
assistance and keen awareness of the academic needs of the students
for whom this course was designed.

The author and publishers would like to thank the following for
permission to reproduce their images:

The Advertising Archives p97
Alamy/Corbis/Nomad p40, Alamy/Corbis/Premium p52(tr), Alamy/
Deco p31, Alamy/Nicolas Duarte p18(tr), Alamy/Paul Fleet p89(bm),
Alamy/I love images p82, Alamy/Imagebroker p33, Alamy/McPhoto/
ADR p25(bl), Alamy/Shapencolour p87, Alamy/Somos Images p42(br),
Alamy/Jeremy Sutton-Hibbert p71, Alamy/Kevin Walsh p57
Axiom /Tim Draper/Rough Guides p99

Corbis/Ingo Arndt/Minden Pictures p60(flying fox), Corbis/Gaetan
Bally/Keystone p21, Corbis/Bettmann p24, Corbis/Tibor Bognar
p67, Corbis/Andrew Brookes p17, Corbis/Demotix p7, Corbis/Laura
Doss p106, Corbis/Patrick Eckersley p80(cr), Corbis/Randy Faris
p52(br), Corbis/FBP/Tetra Images p42(bl), Corbis/Thom Gourley
p75, Corbis/Leon Harris/Cultura p45, Corbis/Jon Hicks p70(br),
Corbis/David Howells p103, Corbis/Sung-Il Kim p25(tl), Corbis/
Brooks Kraft p27, Corbis/Stephanie Kuykendal p50, Corbis/C. Lyttle
p39, Corbis/Magictorch/Ikon Images p47, Corbis/Matt Moyer p37,
Corbis/Gerald Nowak p60(prawn), Corbis/Ocean pp62, 88, Corbis/
Tim Pannell pp69, 73, 102, Corbis/Norbert Schaefer p89(br), Corbis/
David Selman p23, Corbis/Radius Images p90, Corbis/Rick Gayle
Studio p89(bl), Corbis/Robin Skjoldborg/cultura p80(br), Corbis/
Sylvain Sonnet p55(tr), Corbis/Mark Weiss p77, Corbis/Jeremy
Woodhouse p55(tl),
Digital Vision pp48, 60(snail)
FotoLibra/Barbara Domanska   p94, FotoLibra/Matthew Grant
p55(br), FotoLibra/Pene Kelleher p78, FotoLibra/David Knowles
p35, FotoLibra/Andy Myatt p55(bl)
Getty Images pp9(tr), 41, Getty Images/Absodels RM p86, Getty
Images/Amana Images p80(tr), Getty Images/Simon Battensby p92,
Getty Images/Brand X p46, Getty Images/Cultura RF p105(cr), Getty
Images/Design Pics p12, Getty Images/Eightfish p59, Getty Images/
Mark Evans p25(br), Getty Images/First Light p65, Getty Images/
Flickr RM p8, Getty Images/Natalie Fobes p20, Getty Images/fstop
p13, Getty Images/Tim Hawley p25(tr), Getty Images/Harry Hook
p61, Getty Images/Imagenavi p26, Getty Images/Image Source p54,
Getty Images/Johnny Johnson p105(bm), Getty Images/Justin Lewis
p15, Getty Images/Photononstop RM p95, Getty Images/Rubberball
p81, Getty Images/Science Photo Library p28, Getty Images/
SuperStock p49, Getty Images/Topical Press Agency p22, Getty
Images/David Trood/Photonica p66, Getty Images/Visuals Unlimited
p58
Intellectual Property Office/Crown Copyright p18
Oxford University/Department of Zoology p30
Photodisc p9(br)
Science Photo Library pp10, 29, 60(tr), 100
Sun Life Financial/Courtesy of Sun Life Financial p70(tr)

The author(s) and publishers are grateful for permission to reprint the
following copyright material:

Material from 'The Study Skills Handbook' by author Stella Cottrell,
copyright © Stella Cottrell 1999, 2003 & 2008, first published by
Palgrave Macmillan, reproduced with permission of the publisher.

Printed and bound in Thailand

2017 2016 2015 2014 2013
10 9 8 7 6 5 4 3 2 1

Recommended minimum system requirements for the *Skillful* Digibook

Windows

	Windows XP SP3	Vista	Windows 7 & 8
CPU Speed	Core 2 Duo, 2.53 GHz	Core 2 Duo, 2.53 GHz	Core 2 Duo, 2.93 GHz
Browser	Explorer 8 & 9, Firefox, and Chrome		

Macintosh OS

	10.6	10.7	10.8
CPU Speed	Core 2 Duo – 1.83 GHz	Core 2 Duo – 1.83 GHz	Core 2 Duo – 1.83 GHz
Browser	Safari		

Additional recommended minimum system requirements

- Hard Disk (offline version only): Minimum 1 GB free on the install drive and minimum 2 GB free on the system drive.
- Free RAM: 500 MB
- Display: 1024 x 768 pixels, 32-bit colour
- Add-ins: Flash Player 10.1
- Broadband connection: For Authentication/Registration/Download (offline version only)/Updates

Please visit help.macmillan.com for technical support

This software is licensed for use by one user and can be installed on a maximum of one machine.

Product Activation

1 Type *www.skillfuldigibooks.com* into your Internet browser.

2 Click "Enter your token details"

3 You need your access token code, printed on the next page.

4 Type your access token code into the box provided.

5 Follow the step-by-step instructions on the screen to help you register and log-in.

6 You can now use your *Skillful* DigiBook.

Your access token code only allows one user to log in, so don't give yours away, and make sure you use it within one year!